PAUL YOUNG

Recipes found

On my travels

Photography by John Such
Design by Elbury Design

First published in Great Britain in 2012 by Langan & Such Enterprises

© Paul Young, 2012

© John Such, 2012

Photographs © John Such - www.suchgoodpictures.co.uk

Book design & art direction © Richard Elwell - www.elburydesign.com

Archive images © Janet Macoska - www.janetmacoska.com

Back cover photo © Alan Strutt - www.alanstrutt.com

A Special thank you to:

Adrian Derx and his team at Knightor - www.knightor.com

Simon Stallard - www.hiddenhut.co.uk

Wing of St Mawes - www.wingofstmawes.co.uk

Terry Lobb - www.lobbsfarmshop.com

A catalogue record for this book is available from the British Library.

ISBN 978-0-9572741-0-5

GREAT BRITISH BOOKS
PUBLISHED & PRINTED IN THE UK

my thanks go to:

My family, love 'em all, who have been my unwitting tasters over all the years, Ian Kewley for both musical and culinary inspiration, also Marco Pierre White in that respect; my patient managers Mick & David; Stacey, who has even suffered pain whilst helping me; love you, glad the burn on your arm disappeared without trace!

Paul Prudhomme who let me in his kitchen to see what goes on; John and Gregg from Masterchef, James Martin, Gennaro Contaldo, Lawrence Keogh, Barry Vera, all these people and more who were so positive and always wished me well.

Chef Richard McGeown, who was a big help for me in the Knightor kitchen, and his staff Nick & Jake. The Cornwall Collective: John Such, Richard Elwell and Gary Langan, without whom this book would not have got off the ground.

Lastly, but most importantly, all my music fans that have stuck with me over the years; at least you'll know a little more of what I've gotten up to for all of this time!

It was about 18 months ago that photographer John Such contacted me about doing my own cookbook. He had seen me on Celebrity Masterchef and Hell's Kitchen, thought I was serious in my love of food, and thought the idea was a slightly left field surprise for my fans, and anyone else that might be interested. I went away and came up with the first shortlist, and it became obvious that the food choices were influenced by my travels as a musician.

We shot the first few recipes at my house, me cooking manically and John putting his 20 years of experience to good use, but we could tell after our first day that it would take a lifetime to shoot a complete book with me on my lonesome in the kitchen. The idea was put on the back burner for a while until, like a thunderbolt out of the blue, John's business partner Gary Langan came up with the idea of using a professional kitchen and between them they sourced a kitchen, assistants, food suppliers, and we shot 80% of the recipes in 2 days... .

This book may not have been made without John's positive energy, and the occasional kick up the backside I sometimes needed!

on my travels

contents

foreword
James Martin

I first met Paul as a guest on Saturday Kitchen; he had already been on Masterchef so I knew he had a love for food, and as such he was the ideal guest. We share a love for cars and motorbikes too, so the conversation was a mix of love, oil and Duckhams. In fact, we did a motorcycle ride together for a hospital charity with myself and the Hairy Bikers....

Since then Paul has appeared again on the show, and he was also a natural choice to be my guest at the BBC Good Food Show at the NEC Birmingham. So it comes as no surprise that he is bringing out his own cookbook and I hope it's as big a success as his talent behind the microphone. I meet many people in my job who have a love of food but Paul's enthusiasm is genuine and best of all he has the talent to put into practice what he preaches.

I wish him every success and good luck with his new venture and I feel honoured to have Paul as a friend.

my food journey

First and foremost, I have to mention the 'Reverend' Ian
Kewley, keyboard player in the Q-Tips, for my interest in food.
Although he was a classically trained musician, he was also
cooking at his family home from a very early age, and at the
time he was in The Q-Tips with me, he was into Indian food,
and amazing it was too. Once we were sharing my solo success,
he was moving into other styles, and we would always try to
find good local restaurants wherever we were playing. It became
my 'treat' after any punishing schedule to reward ourselves
with a bit of fine dining. His enthusiasm was infectious, and
I started trying to improve my culinary skills at home... .

Over the years, the by-product of being a travelling musician is
the diversity of amazing food it has been my pleasure to taste;
yes, I have even got tearful at some restaurants... I remember
one in Gubbio, Italy where the owner didn't know I was there
for lunch and insisted we come back in the evening, when he
personally would cook for me and my friends. All seven (!) courses
were breathtaking, and his passion moved me so much, well,
you know... .

And sometimes, when I had something that I could honestly
say I wouldn't find back home, I would buy a cookbook from
that region so I could learn how to make it for my friends.
That was when it all started to get serious!

I've always thought that music and food go hand in hand; if you hear music from a certain part of the world, you can sometimes shut your eyes and put yourself there. If you've got the food as well, you're hitting two of the senses, hearing and taste; why, it's almost like a cheap holiday! So a cooking musician is not such an unusual thing, both involve pleasing an audience of sorts; don't they even sometimes say the music is 'really cookin'? And, let's not forget my first taste of a hit was a song called "Toast"... I shoulda seen it coming!

Hence the reason why I found myself on Celebrity Masterchef and Hell's kitchen with Marco Pierre White. Hell, if I'm gonna make a prat of myself on live TV, I might as well learn somethin' from the best!!

So here I am with my first cookbook; the title speaks for itself, 'On My Travels' is precisely that; food I tasted around the world that ignited my taste buds, and that I wanted to make for my friends back home. I've tried to recall when and where I first had it whenever possible, and I've also included a few really simple family favourites that will always come in handy Saying that, I can get just as much enjoyment out of a simple pasta with tomato sauce as I can from some extravagant dish from Mexico, so feel free to stay as simple or as complicated as you want! Enjoy... .

soups

Leek & Potato Soup

Thai Sweet Potato & Coconut Soup

Mexican Corn Chowder

Roast Pumpkin Soup

A family favourite, mainly because they can dress it up how they want to. Children like the simple things, but the older ones can dress it up a little... .

Levi and I add a little hot sauce, parmesan gives it a slight minestrone feel, the other kids like Cheddar cheese on it and you can also blend it, then add a little cream, and garnish with a little more parsley for a Cream of Leek & Potato Soup! And, it's painfully simple ... remember, you're cooking all these fresh ingredients and it takes no more than half an hour in all.

Leek & Potato Soup

Just place all the ingredients into a large saucepan, bring to the boil, cover and simmer for 15 minutes, or until the potatoes are cooked. Simple as that!

INGREDIENTS:

1 onion, very finely chopped

1500ml/50 fl oz/6 cups chicken stock

4 medium potatoes, peeled & diced

4 leeks, sliced

4 tbsps chopped parsley

2 tbsps tomato purée

Black pepper

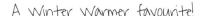
A Winter Warmer favourite!

Thai Sweet Potato & Coconut Soup

INGREDIENTS:

Olive oil

1 onion, chopped

1 celery stick, rough chopped

1 carrot, rough chopped

2 cloves garlic (optional)

1" fresh ginger, peeled and grated

1 red thai chili, chopped

3-4 orange flesh sweet potatoes, depending on size

About 2 cups/¾ pint/450ml of chicken stock

1x 14oz/400ml tin of coconut milk

Juice of ½ lime

Fresh chopped coriander

Salt & pepper to taste

In a large pot, pour a couple of tablespoons of olive oil and on medium heat, add the chopped onion, celery and carrot. After a couple of minutes, add the garlic, ginger and chili and sweat for about 5-6 minutes with the lid on. To help them sweat, you could tear some greaseproof paper and push it down on top of the ingredients before you put the lid on.

Take off the paper, add the sweet potatoes and stir to coat in the oil and ingredients for about 5 more minutes. Add the stock, which should always just cover all the ingredients to get the right consistency for this soup, cover and simmer until the potatoes are soft.

Take off the heat, blend in a processor, or blender if you like but not for too long, then return to the pot. Add the coconut milk and bring back to the boil, tasting for seasoning. Lastly, add the juice of ½ a lime and a handful of chopped coriander and serve, with a drizzle of extra virgin olive oil and a pinch of chili flakes.

A winter warmer... I've gotten more into soups of late, particularly when the Halloween / Bonfire Night / Christmas season starts, and this is a good one.

Mexican Corn Chowder

INGREDIENTS: *Serves 4*

¼ lb/125g butter

½ cup/150g/5oz sliced mushrooms

1 green bell pepper, diced

1 large onion, diced

1 jalapeno chili, diced

1 tsp cumin seed

¾ cup/90g/6oz plain flour

1 tsp ground paprika

1 tsp ground red pepper

1 quart/1 litre/4 cups chicken stock

2 cups/500 ml/16fl oz pouring cream

½ cup/75g/2½ oz grated Cheddar cheese

17oz/500g tinned sweetcorn

1 tbsp chopped fresh parsley

1 tbsp diced pimiento peppers

Salt

Heat a large saucepan over medium heat, add 2 tablespoons of the butter and sauté the mushrooms until they're browned, about 3 to 4 minutes, remove, and reserve them.

Add the remaining butter to the saucepan; add the bell pepper, onion, jalapeno and cumin seed and sauté until they're soft, about 3 to 5 minutes. Whisk in the flour, paprika and red pepper and mix well to eliminate any lumps that may form.

Reduce the heat to low, stir in the chicken stock, and mix well. Add the pouring cream and the cheese and stir continuously until the cheese has melted and the soup has thickened.

Add the corn, parsley, pimiento and the reserved mushrooms; mix well and heat thoroughly. Salt to taste and serve immediately.

A Halloween favourite; we get through quite a few pumpkins, with 4 large ones to decorate and put on the window sill, and another 4 for this dish, as I make quadruple the amount shown here!

Roast Pumpkin Soup

Pre-heat the oven to 180ºC/350"F/Gas Mark 4. Place the whole pumpkin or butternut squashes in the oven and roast for 1½ hours until soft.

Halve the pumpkin or butternut squashes, scoop out the seeds and fibres, and discard. Scoop the flesh from the skin and place in a large bowl.

Place the oil in a deep saucepan and stir in the onion, celery, carrot, garlic and bay leaf. Cover the vegetables directly with some greaseproof paper, put the lid on and sweat for about 10-15 minutes.

Stir the roasted pumpkin or squash flesh into the vegetables together with the stock (always enough to cover the vegetables), season with salt & pepper, bring to the boil then simmer until the vegetables are tender.

Discard the bay leaf and transfer the soup to a food processor. Process until smooth. Return the soup to the pan and heat through, adjusting the seasoning for the last time. Serve in bowls with lots of warm bread.

INGREDIENTS:

1 medium pumpkin, about 1kg (2¼lb), or 2 medium butternut squashes

30ml, approx 2 tbsps of olive oil

1 onion, peeled and chopped

2 celery sticks, trimmed and chopped

1 carrot, peeled and chopped

3 garlic cloves, peeled and chopped

1 bay leaf

1.2 litres (2 pints) chicken stock

Salt and freshly ground black pepper

15g (½ oz) butter

breakfasts & starters

Poached Eggs on Butternut Squash Hash

Huevos Rancheros

Huevos Habaneras
Havana Style Eggs

Ceviche

Pan Roasted Soft-Shell Crabs

Smoked Trout Mousse

Vitello Tonnato
Veal in Tuna Fish Sauce

I love an English breakfast as much as the next man, but it's nice to have an alternative up your sleeve (note: I love to fry a quartered banana in the bacon fat and lay it on top of the bacon in your English breakfast; try it!).

I'm loving squashes and pumpkins in my cooking at the moment, hence this idea...

Poached Eggs on Butternut Squash Hash

Boil 4 cups / 2 pints / 1 ltr water in medium saucepan. Add squash & potatoes. Cover & part boil (approx 4 minutes) until almost tender. Drain & reserve.

In a frying pan on medium-high heat, add oil, bacon & onion and cook for approx 3 minutes, or until bacon is almost cooked. Add squash & potato and season, then cook for a further 5 minutes, stirring occasionally.

Add sage and cook until the vegetables are brown and the bacon is crispy, about 5 minutes. At that same time bring a pot of water to the boil, add salt and vinegar, then poach the eggs, for approx 3 minutes.

Serve with a poached egg on top of a mound of hash, divided equally between four plates, and decorate with a couple of sage leaves.

INGREDIENTS:

3 cups ¼" diced butternut squash, peeled & seeded (use a tea mug!)

2 medium potatoes, ¼" diced

Olive oil

4 strips bacon, cut into ¼" strips

1 medium white/yellow onion, diced

6 sage leaves chopped coarsely, or 1 tsp dried

2 tbsps vinegar

4 eggs

Salt & pepper

INGREDIENTS: *Serves 4*

Roasted Tomato Salsa:

1½lb/750g plum tomatoes

2 New Mexico green chilies

2 garlic cloves, unpeeled

1 small white onion, diced

2 tsps vegetable oil

2 tsps cider vinegar

1 tsp sugar

¼ tsp ground cumin

¼ tsp dried oregano

1 tbsp lime juice

Salt

Huevos Rancheros:

Vegetable oil

4 corn tortillas

4 eggs

Grated Cheddar cheese

30 breakfasts

Mexican breakfast! I always used to order this when we played in Texas, or anywhere in the South West. It's basically tortillas, eggs and salsa, but there are a number of variations. If I've pre-made some black beans, I'll definitely put some on the side with the salsa; the eggs can be fried and placed on the sauce; and the salsa can be homemade or prepared — although I like the idea of making this cooked variation of tomato salsa, different to the raw salsa shown in this book.

Huevos Rancheros

To make the roasted tomato salsa, place the tomatoes, chilies and garlic on a baking sheet under the grill, and roast them until their skins blister and blacken, checking and turning them frequently. Allow the vegetables to cool. Peel and chop the tomatoes, seed and dice the chilies, and mince the garlic.

Then, in a saucepan over medium heat, sauté the onion in the oil until it's soft but not going brown. Add the roasted vegetables, vinegar, sugar, cumin and oregano and simmer for 3 to 4 minutes to release the tomato juices and thicken the sauce (if you've used tinned plum tomatoes, you may have to cook them a little longer). Add the lime juice, season with the salt, and simmer for another couple of minutes.

Pour the oil in a frying pan to a depth of 1" (2½ cm) and heat it over a high flame. When the oil is very hot, make a small slit in the centre of a tortilla so that it doesn't puff up, and fry it for a few seconds until it's crisp. Remove it from the oil, drain it on paper towels, and repeat the procedure with the remaining tortillas. Put them on a plate in an oven on low heat to keep warm. Now pour off all but a teaspoon of the oil.

Break the eggs into the frying pan and fry them to desired doneness. To present the dish, place a tortilla on each plate and spoon on some of the salsa. Put the eggs on top of the salsa, garnish with the cheese, add a couple more spoonfuls of the salsa on the side and serve immediately, with the blue corn muffins if you made them!

First a Mexican style breakfast, now a Cuban style breakfast! It's a nice way to serve eggs, and all healthy stuff. Serve with crusty bread and fresh coffee.

Preheat oven to 180°C/350ºF/Gas Mark 4.

Sauté the onion, red and green bell pepper in the olive oil over low heat until the onions are translucent. Add the garlic and cook a few minutes more, stirring occasionally. Add the tomatoes, wine, and cumin and cook over low heat for about five minutes, stirring frequently.

Salt & pepper to taste.

Lightly oil four ramekins and put a good couple of tablespoons of the mixture in each. Gently break two eggs into each dish on top (be careful not to break the yolks!). Place one tablespoon of butter on top of the eggs in each dish.

Place the dishes in the oven and bake for 12 minutes or so (less if the eggs are small): until the whites are white and cooked. The yolks should be slightly runny. Sprinkle a little paprika on top to season and serve immediately.

Huevos Habaneras

Havana Style Eggs

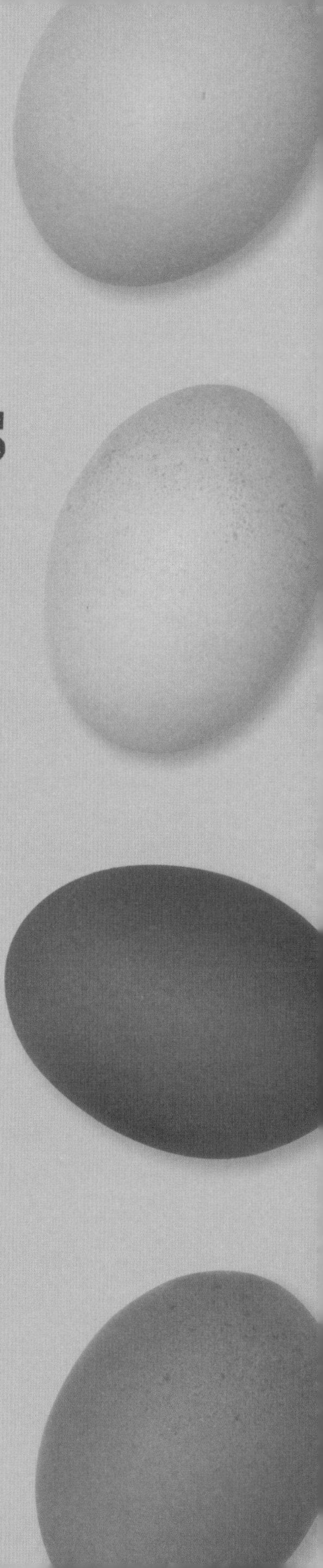

INGREDIENTS:

2 tbsps olive oil for frying

1 large onion, finely chopped

1 medium green pepper, chopped

1 medium red pepper, chopped

3 cloves garlic finely chopped

1 cup/4 fresh plum tomatoes, deseeded and chopped

2 tbsps white wine

½ tsp cumin

Salt & pepper, to taste

8 medium eggs

4 tbsps unsalted butter

Paprika to season

This is a South American dish, great at lunchtime; once again, we find that recipes vary from country to country. In Mexico they like to use mackerel, probably the most traditional fish to use. But, as it's my book, I find mackerel disintegrates too quickly. Fine, maybe, if you're in a restaurant and you can serve it almost as soon as the fish comes out of the fridge and is prepared, but leave it much longer and the lime juice starts to break the fish up and it starts to look too congealed and not very kind on the eye. The acidic juice of the lime 'cooks' the fish.

I tried monkfish, too, but it's a tougher fish and a bit chewy for my palate.

So I'm going with snapper or mullet. Still, it won't really last, so it's all got to be eaten when served, really.

Ceviche

Chop the fish into half inch pieces, put into a deep glass bowl and pour over the lime (preferable) or lemon juice, making sure it covers the fish. Cover & refrigerate for about 6 hours, turning the fish once in the process.

Drain the fish and keep the juice.

Put the fish into a serving dish, add the remaining ingredients (not the olives) together with the lime juice and pour over the fish.

You can refrigerate again, but take out of the fridge a short while before serving. Add the olives as a garnish. And of course, some bread to soak up the sauce, and a glass of white to help it down…! Then a siesta….

INGREDIENTS:

450g/1lb fillets of red snapper or red mullet

350ml/12 fl oz/1½ cups of lime or lemon juice, enough to cover the fish

225g/8oz tomatoes, chopped and de-seeded

1 onion, finely sliced

2 pickled jalapeno chilies, rinsed & chopped

50ml/2 fl oz/¼ cup olive oil

1 tbsp white vinegar

2 tbsps chopped coriander

¼ tsp dried oregano

Salt

Green olives

Pan Roasted Soft-Shell Crabs

FOR THE MANGO CHUTNEY:

1 tsp black mustard seeds

1 tsp black peppercorns

1 tsp cumin seeds

1 tsp dried chili flakes

1 tsp coriander seeds

2 ripe mangoes, cut into ½" squares

1 greener mango, cut into ½" squares

125g/4 ½ oz light soft brown sugar

110ml/4fl oz malt vinegar

SEASONING MIX:

¾ tsp onion powder

¾ tsp black pepper

¾ tsp salt

½ tsp dried basil

½ tsp cayenne

½ tsp dried mustard

½ tsp paprika

¼ tsp star anise

¼ tsp garlic powder

¼ tsp white pepper

I first had soft-shell crabs at The Ivy, a famous restaurant in Los Angeles, which serves food heavily influenced by Cajun cuisine. They have much larger soft-shells in the U.S. than the ones available here in the UK (of course), and they serve two as a starter! I could never get through the main course after that... I would suggest just one as a starter, or two for a main course, much more manageable.

Surprisingly, most good fishmongers will have perfectly acceptable frozen soft-shell crabs in stock, though it would be advisable to check first. And yes, you eat the whole thing!

Heat a frying pan until hot. Add all of the spices and toast for 30 seconds, or until the mustard seeds start to pop. Transfer to a mortar and pestle and rough grind the seeds. Transfer back to the frying pan. Add the green mango and ripe mangoes and cook for 1-2 minutes. Add the sugar and cook until dissolved into the mango juices, and then add the vinegar.

Cover the mango mixture and reduce the heat to simmer for 25 minutes, or until the mango has broken down and the mixture resembles chutney. Place half of the chutney mixture into a food processor and blend to a purée, then return to the pan and mix with the remaining unblended chutney. Pour the chutney into sterilized jars and allow to cool a little before serving.

Combine the seasoning mix ingredients in a small bowl.

Preheat the oven to 350°F.

INGREDIENTS:

6 soft-shell crabs

4 tbsps unsalted butter

Sprinkle the crabs evenly with 3 to 5 teaspoons of the seasoning mix, according to your own taste, and gently pat it in.

Melt the butter in a large ovenproof frying pan. When it begins to sizzle, place the crabs in the pan, top side down. Cook, turning once, until the crabs are brown on both sides, about 3 to 4 minutes per side. Place the pan in the oven (Make sure you don't have a plastic handle! Otherwise transfer to a bakeproof dish). Bake until the crabs are cooked through and the shells are slightly crisp, about 20 minutes.

To serve, place a couple of dessert spoonfuls of the mango on the plate and place a crab on top of the chutney.

A sneakily easy dish to prepare. Although all the ingredients look daunting, bear in mind that you've got 3 main parts: 1) the smoked trout and 2) the cream cheese are ready to go straight into the processor. All the other ingredients are done together, in about 20 minutes, left to cool, and then put in as the third main part and blended together.

INGREDIENTS:

2 tbsps olive oil

1 cup chopped onions (use a coffee mug)

¼ cup seeded, chopped green bell peppers

¼ cup seeded, chopped red bell peppers

¼ cup seeded, chopped yellow bell peppers

2 tbsps unsalted butter

2 tsps peeled and minced fresh ginger

1 tsp minced fresh garlic

1 tbsp freshly squeezed lemon juice

1 tbsp freshly squeezed lime juice

1 tbsp lightly packed light brown sugar

½ cup/4fl oz/125ml seafood stock

12oz/350g cream cheese, softened

12oz/350g smoked trout

SEASONING MIX:

1¼ tsps salt

1¼ tsps paprika

1 tsp ground ginger

1 tsp dry mustard

1 tsp onion powder

¾ tsp ground anise

¾ tsp dried basil

¾ tsp cayenne pepper

¾ tsp garlic powder

¾ tsp ground ancho chili peppers

¾ tsp ground New Mexico chili pepper

½ tsp white pepper

Smoked Trout Mousse

Combine the seasoning mix ingredients in a small bowl.

Heat the olive oil in a heavy 10 inch frying pan, preferably non-stick, over high heat just until the oil begins to smoke, about 3 to 4 minutes. Add the onions, all the bell peppers, and 2 tablespoons of the seasoning mix. Stir well and cook, stirring and scraping the bottom of the pan frequently, until the vegetables begin to brown on the edges, about 4 to 6 minutes. The vegetables should just begin to darken from the heat and seasoning mix and still be slightly crunchy. Add the butter, ginger, and garlic and stir until the butter melts. Add the citrus juices and brown sugar and continue to cook, stirring frequently, until the juices are almost evaporated, about 4 to 5 minutes. Stir in the stock, scrape the bottom of the pan to loosen all the brown material on the bottom, then add the remaining seasoning mix. Stir well and continue to cook, stirring frequently, until the mixture thickens a bit, about 3 to 4 minutes. Remove from the heat; transfer to a sheet pan and refrigerate until cold.

In a food processor combine the vegetable mixture with the cream cheese and smoked trout. Process until the mixture is fairly smooth, about 1 minute.

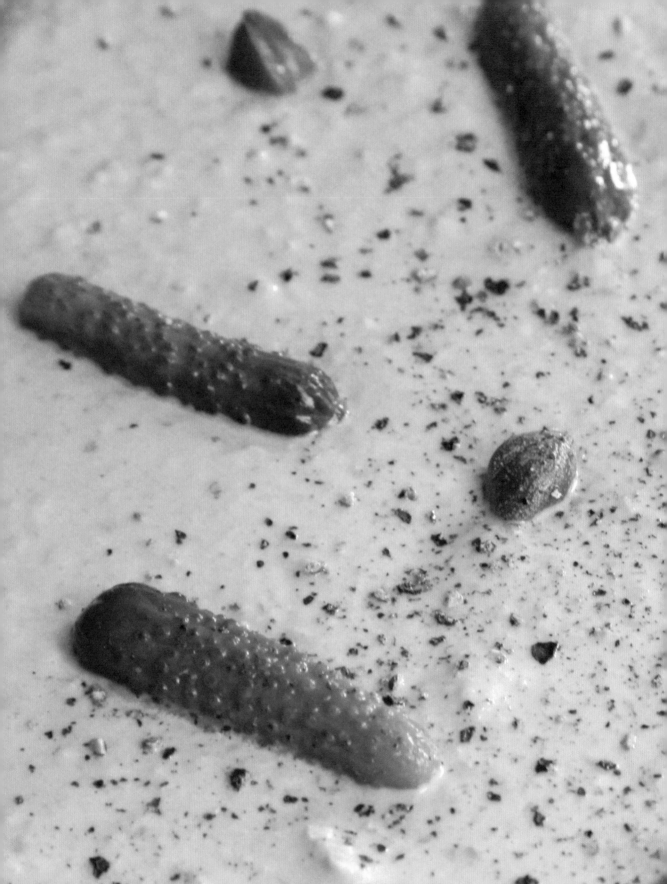

I included this because although we've been going to Italian restaurants in the UK for decades, I'm amazed at the amount of people who don't know what this is! Putting meat with fish seems strange, but they complement each other perfectly, and it's a lovely light lunch plate. This is a generous amount though, for a starter; it would serve about 10 people. You could cook a smaller piece of meat if it's part of mixed antipasti, but still make the same amount of sauce and use it up on toast! Veal is easier to find these days, as the old myths about veal are laid to rest even as the farming of veal improves... .

Vitello Tonnato
Veal in Tuna Fish Sauce

INGREDIENTS: *Serves 4*

1kg/2lb of veal steak (silverside or topside)

1 carrot, chopped

A couple of celery stalks, cut in pieces

1 onion

170g/6oz tuna fish in oil

2 tbsp capers, plus a few extra for decoration

6 anchovy fillets, fresh if possible

150g/6 fl oz/¾ cups fresh mayonnaise

A few gherkin pickles for decoration

Salt & freshly ground black pepper

Put the meat together with the pieces of carrot, celery and onion and a pinch of salt into boiling water for around one hour. Leave to cool, then cut the veal into very thin slices and arrange on a dish. As it's best at about 1mm thick, it may be worth going back to the butcher if you don't have a slicing machine; I do.

Put the vegetables together with the tuna, capers and anchovies through the food processor to produce the consistency of a thick paste. You may need to push the ingredients down with a spatula and re-process. Then add the mayonnaise, a little salt & pepper and process again. Spread the paste over the veal slices and decorate with a few gherkins and capers.

pasta & risotto

Fettuccini
with Cream Parmesan Sauce

Risotto con Porcini
Mushroom Risotto

Bucatini alla Carbonara

Tomato Sauce

Pumpkin Risotto

Pappardelle with Venison
and Chestnut Sauce

Penne with Fig Sauce

Lemon & Basil Spaghetti

Risotto con Asparagi

This is more than a little on the rich side! I had this in New Orleans first, but when I'm making a pasta tricolore (a choice of 3 pastas with red, green and white sauces, like the Italian flag), I'll use this as the white sauce alongside pesto and tomato based sauces. On it's own, though, I'd have a small plate of it with a green salad drizzled in olive oil and balsamic vinegar just to break it down a bit.

Fettuccini
with Cream Parmesan Sauce

Bring a large pot of salted water to the boil.

Melt the butter on low heat in a frying pan; just before it has all melted, add the cayenne pepper and the cream.

Raise the heat a bit and bring to the boil, whisking constantly.

Reduce the heat and simmer for about 7-8 minutes.

Take off the heat and add the Parmesan gradually, whisking it in. Set aside.

Drop the fresh fettuccini in the boiling water for about 3 minutes, then drain and toss in a little vegetable or olive oil to stop it sticking.

Add the sauce to the fettuccini and mix well. Serve.

INGREDIENTS:

½lb/225g fresh fettuccini

6oz/170g unsalted butter

2 cups/15fl oz/450ml pouring cream

½ tsp cayenne pepper

½ cup/4oz/125g grated Parmesan cheese

A little veg or olive oil

Salt & pepper

Risotto con Porcini
Mushroom Risotto

Gently clean the ceps or other mushrooms, using a sharp knife and a brush (avoid washing them whenever possible). If you are using dried ceps, put them to soak in a small bowl of water for 15 minutes. Meanwhile, slice the fresh ceps or mushrooms.

Put a large saucepan over medium heat, add the oil and butter and when almost melted, add the finely chopped onion. When the onion begins to colour, add the sliced ceps and continue to fry over a moderate flame for a couple of minutes. If using the dried ceps, chop them into small pieces and add to the mushrooms, keeping the water they soaked in to add to the risotto later with the stock. Add the rice and stir into the mix. Then slowly add the mushroom water, followed by the chicken stock, stirring all the time. Add each next ladleful when the rice is getting sticky in the pan.

When the rice is al dente, remove from the heat, season, and stir in a teaspoon of butter and the Parmesan cheese.

Prepare a mound of risotto in the middle of a bowl, or plate, drizzle a little olive oil and balsamic around the mound for decoration and place some shaved Parmesan on the top.

INGREDIENTS:
350g/12oz small fresh ceps, or button mushrooms
25g/1oz dried ceps
1 small finely chopped onion
2tbsp olive oil
Balsamic glaze
30g/1oz/2tbsp butter
350g/12oz arborio rice
1½ litres/3pt chicken stock, kept warm
Salt & fresh ground black pepper
60g/2oz/½ cup grated Parmesan cheese, and some shavings

This is often done with spaghetti, but I think
with such a hearty, breakfast kind of sauce,
it's better suited to the bigger, meatier size of
bucatini. It's like hollow, fat spaghetti and worth
looking for... .

Bucatini alla Carbonara

Cook the bucatini in boiling salted water, following packet directions carefully to avoid overcooking.

While the pasta is cooking, beat the eggs and cream together with a pinch of salt. Heat the oil and butter in a pan. Add the bacon strips and cook gently until the fat becomes transparent, then take off the heat.

Drain the pasta; add the bacon in its oil to the pasta pot and pour the drained pasta back. Stir well. Remove the pan from the heat and stir in the beaten eggs and cream and a small quantity of the cheese.

The eggs will start to bind, or cook as they come into contact with the hot pasta so it is very important to work quickly. Stir until each strand of pasta is coated with a thick yellow cream. Now stir in the rest of the cheese and freshly ground black pepper to taste. Serve at once with even more black pepper and Parmesan!

INGREDIENTS:
500g/1lb bucatini

5 eggs

100ml/4 fl oz/½ cup double or heavy cream

Salt and black pepper

1tbsp olive oil

2tbsp butter

200g/7oz pancetta or thick cut bacon, cut into strips

100g/4oz/1¼ cups freshly grated Parmesan and pecorino romano cheese, preferably half and half

Why my basic tomato sauce? Well, the only thing I stress here is the amount you reduce the sauce; this is where the sauce goes from any other tomato sauce, to special. You've got to reduce it a bit further than you'd think. Somewhere in the 15-20 minutes, the sauce achieves a much more concentrated tomato taste than before; at that point, take it off the heat.

My Basic
Tomato Sauce

Heat the olive oil in a frying pan. Bring a big pot of salted water to the boil. On medium heat, add the onions and sweat for a minute. Add the garlic for another 30 seconds to a minute. Add the cans of plum tomatoes. Add the sugar, then add salt & pepper to taste. Bring to a boil, then go back to medium heat to reduce the sauce for about 15-20 minutes (see above).

Remove from the heat and let it cool a little while you add the pasta to the water. My kids love penne the best, but occasionally they'll go for spaghetti. Whatever, follow the instructions for boiling time, but test when it gets close, to make sure the pasta doesn't go beyond 'al dente'. You can't go back! Blend or process the sauce, and add to your pasta.

You could also put the sauce back in the frying pan, add a few basil leaves and heat gently for a slightly different flavour to your sauce.

You could also gently sweat some bacon strips in a little oil, a teaspoon of butter, and half a teaspoon of chili flakes, pour that over the penne then add some of your tomato sauce, and you've got an all' amatriciana sauce. The possibilities are endless... .

INGREDIENTS:

Olive oil

1 medium to large onion, chopped

1 clove garlic, chopped (optional)

2 x 14oz cans of plum tomatoes

1 tsp of sugar

Salt & pepper

We have thrown the biggest Halloween parties in our area, particularly when the kids were younger. We saw how much the kids enjoyed it when I was working in Los Angeles, and wanted to do the same back home. This is a favourite to do on Halloween, more for the parents than the children.

Pumpkin Risotto

Heat the oil and half the butter in a large saucepan, add the shallots and fry gently for 5 minutes, until soft. Stir in the pumpkin or squash with the garlic and cook for about 8 minutes, until it starts to soften. Bring the stock to a simmer in a separate pan. Meanwhile, stir the rice into the pumpkin, making sure each grain is glistening with butter. Add the wine and cook for 2 minutes, until it has evaporated.

Add a ladleful of hot stock to the rice and cook over a moderate heat, stirring for 3-5 minutes until it has been absorbed. Continue adding the stock a ladleful at a time, always stirring, until nearly all the stock has been used, then test to see if the rice and the pumpkin are tender. The rice should have a tiny bit of bite left in the grain.

Then, remove from the heat and stir in the last remaining butter, the parsley, and the Parmesan cheese.

INGREDIENTS:

2 tbsps extra virgin olive oil

50g/2oz butter

6 shallots, finely chopped

450g/1lb pumpkin or butternut squash, peeled, seeded and cut into 1cm (½in) cubes

2 garlic cloves, crushed

1.5 litres/3 pt chicken (preferred) or vegetable stock

350g/12oz good quality risotto rice

120ml/4fl oz dry white wine

3 tbsps chopped fresh flat-leaf parsley

4 tbsps freshly grated Parmesan cheese

Salt & freshly ground black pepper

Although Italians regularly use venison, the taste of that meat and the berries always puts me in Scandinavia, the first place I had venison for Christmas dinner. Put it on pasta though, and I'm reminded of a ski lunch in the Italian Alps! With a sauce like this, the broader the pasta the better. I know that sometimes the thickest pasta you'll find in your local supermarket would be tagliatelle, in which case go with it. Spaghetti, though, just won't do... .

Pappardelle with Venison
and Chestnut Sauce

In a large frying pan, heat the olive oil over medium heat. Add the venison, sprinkle with the salt and juniper berries, and stir. Cook until the venison is evenly browned all over. When the juice from the venison has evaporated, add the onion and cranberry sauce, stir and cook for a few more minutes. Stir in the flour and chestnuts. Raise the heat to medium-high, and deglaze the pan with the red wine and the tomato paste. Cook until the liquid in the pan has been almost absorbed, then pour in the stock, lower the heat and simmer for approximately 20 minutes, or until the venison is tender and the sauce is reduced to a gravy consistency that will cling to the pasta. Take off the heat and add the butter.

Cook the pasta in plenty of salted boiling water for the allotted time on the pasta instructions. Drain, toss with the sauce in the pan, and serve hot. Enough for 4 people.

INGREDIENTS:

6 tbsps extra virgin olive oil

680g/1½ lb lean venison, trimmed and cut into ¼" cubes

Salt & pepper as needed

8 juniper berries, crushed

2 medium onions, finely chopped

2 tbsps cranberry sauce

2 tbsps flour

8 chestnuts, shelled and crumbled/finely chopped

1 cup red wine

2 tbsps tomato paste

4 cups vegetable stock

2 tbsps unsalted butter

Enough pappardelle for 6 people

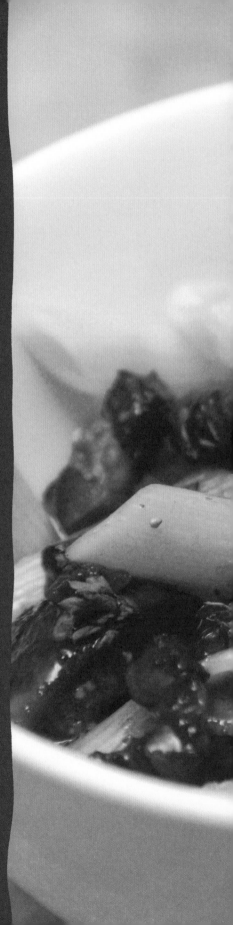

This is something I thought of one day at home; the idea of figs with pasta, also the combination of figs with bacon. This serves two, so double everything up if need be... .

Penne with Fig Sauce

Bring a large pan of salted water to the boil. Add the penne now, as the sauce can be made in the time it takes for dried penne to cook.

Heat the oil in a medium saucepan, add the garlic until it starts to brown, then add the bacon and fry until the bacon goes translucent, stirring now and then. Add the chopped figs and the half glass of red wine and let it simmer gently for a few minutes. Now add the balsamic vinegar and the cream, stir well and reduce the sauce a little. Drain the pasta and stir a couple of spoonfuls of sauce into it, then serve the pasta with more sauce over the top.

INGREDIENTS:

Penne pasta

Extra virgin olive oil

1 clove garlic

100g/3½oz smoked bacon, chopped, or pancetta affumicata

6 ripe figs, chopped

½ glass of red wine

A few drops of balsamic vinegar

½ tsp chili flakes

1 dessertspoon of cream

Lemon & Basil Spaghetti

Cook the spaghetti in a generous amount of boiling salted water, then drain thoroughly and return to the saucepan.

Meanwhile, beat the lemon juice with the olive oil, and then stir in the parmesan until thick and creamy. The parmesan will melt into the mixture. Season, and add more or less lemon juice to taste.

Add the sauce to the spaghetti, and shake the pan so that each strand is coated with the cheese. Finally, stir in the chopped basil and, ideally, some grated lemon zest.

INGREDIENTS:
250g/9oz spaghetti
Sea salt and freshly ground black pepper
Juice of 3-4 lemons
150ml/5fl oz/ 2/3 cup olive oil
150g/5oz/ 2/3 cup parmesan, freshly grated
2 handfuls fresh basil leaves, finely chopped

Risotto con Asparagi

Asparagus Risotto

A good vegetarian option for friends, and a favourite of mine... .

INGREDIENTS:

500g/1lb fresh green asparagus

1.5 litres/3 pt water (for cooking asparagus and for risotto)

2 veg stock cubes

1 small onion, finely chopped

60g/2oz/4tbsp butter

350g/12oz arborio rice

60g/2oz/½ cup Parmesan cheese

Salt and fresh ground black pepper

Rocket leaves

Balsamic vinegar (reduced)

Parmesan shavings

Wash and peel the asparagus and cut away 3cm (1 good inch) or so of the hard white stalk at the bottom (use this and the skin to add flavour to the cooking water). Cut off about 5 cm (2 inches) of the tips and set them aside (as they are tender they will need less cooking) and keep them intact for decoration. Boil the asparagus stalks with the skins and scraps in 1.5 litres (3 pts) water to which you have added the stock cubes. When they are almost cooked add the tips, so that they blanch. When the stalks are fully cooked strain the stock and keep it simmering. Separate out the asparagus tips and stalks. Set the tips aside for decoration, but chop the stalks finely.

Fry the onion in half the butter, then add the chopped asparagus and toss it for a couple of minutes. Now add the rice and proceed as for the basic risotto method, adding the broth until the rice is al dente and creamy but not too solid with asparagus sauce. Remove from the heat and wait for a minute or two, then stir in the remaining butter and the freshly grated Parmesan cheese.

Just before serving, rough chop a good 2 handfuls of rocket leaves and stir into the risotto. In a large bowl, put a decent mound of risotto in the centre and stack four or five of the tips on top (to make the tips go a little further you could slice them lengthways). Shave some fresh Parmesan on top, then drizzle some reduced balsamic vinegar over and serve.

meat

Puerco Pibil

Pollo Mole

Stuffed Pork Chops

Steak Tagliata

Carne Asada

Venison Red Chile

Nut-Coated Chicken Breast
with Mustard Sauce

I saw this recipe put to good use in the Robert Rodriguez movie, Once Upon A Time In Mexico. It's a traditional dish, and I've kept to the guidelines put out by Robert himself here.

Puerco Pibil

INGREDIENTS:

For the achiote paste:

5 tbsps annatto seeds

1 tbsp black peppercorns

2 tsps cumin seeds

½ tsp cloves

8 whole allspice

For the marinade:

2 habanero peppers, de-seeded and de-veined

½ cup/4fl oz/125ml orange juice

½ cup/4fl oz/125ml white vinegar

2 tbsps salt

8 cloves garlic

5 lemons

Big splash of fine tequila

5lbs pork rump

Banana leaves

In a coffee grinder, grind the achiote paste ingredients finely. If you use dried habaneros, add them to the grinder too.

In a blender, add the achiote, habanero peppers, OJ, white vinegar, salt & garlic and blend thoroughly. Add the juice of 5 lemons and tequila.

Dice the pork butt into 2" squares, put into a zip-up freezer bag, add the marinade and close; shake thoroughly and put into the fridge. Alternatively, put into a non-metallic bowl, clingfilm and put in the fridge to marinate for at least 2 hours.

In a deep oven dish, put some banana leaves in the bottom, add the marinated pork and put more banana leaves over the top.

Cover snugly with tin foil and roast in the oven for 4 hours at 325ºF/160ºC, gas mark 3, for about 3-4 hours.

This is maybe too much for a meal if you're splitting it with the Poblano Mole, so you can half the recipe... .

This is my favorite sauce to make; it takes time, but it's unlike anything I've tasted before, so I frequently make it for my friends to try.

Beware that it is an acquired taste, and quite rich. So I always prepare another Mexican dish, for example the Puerco Pibil, together with some guacamole and rice.

Pollo Mole

So take a lazy day to make this! The recipe is in 3 parts essentially, so I prep the ingredients in the morning (up until everything is blended); then I put the TV on while I strain the ingredients through the strainer as it takes about 15-20 mins!

Then relax and watch the film; then late afternoon I start making the sauce from the ingredients, ready to cook the chicken (traditionally it's with turkey and called Poblano Mole, but chicken has more flavor). There is plenty of sauce here so I split what's left into freezable containers for use later. It should keep for a couple of months.

As this is a Mexican recipe, the text is American; but for bell pepper, read sweet pepper, tomatillos are green tomatoes (no, not unripe reds! They have a sharper taste), and plantains you should find in Asian shops, hopefully also the tomatillos. While you're there, if they've got banana leaves, buy 'em and freeze 'em! Good for presentation on this dish, also for the Puerco Pibil.

One other thing; don't despair over the amount of sugar. This is what puts this recipe above all the others I tried. You've got a lot of bitterness to offset, from the bitter Mexican chocolate to the dry toasted/fried dried chilies, also the tartness of the tomatillos and keep tasting! Too little is not enough, but too much and you can't go back.

Preheat an oven to 350°F/180C/Gas mark 4

Clean any dust and dirt from the dried chilies with a damp towel and dry them off thoroughly. If the chilies are moist during the dry sautéing, they will char and be bitter. Stem all the chilies but do not seed. Set aside.

Roast the red bell pepper in the oven, then stem and peel only, do not seed. Set aside.

Place the sesame seeds in a dry medium size frying pan over low heat. Stir the seeds or shake the pan constantly until the seeds are slightly brown, 20 minutes or so. Be careful not to burn them. Remove from the heat and empty into a good-sized bowl to cool. Reserve 3 tablespoons of the browned seeds for garnish.

In a large, dry frying pan over low heat, place the chipotle, ancho/mulato and pasilla negro chilies, and shake the pan constantly or stir until they are evenly toasted, 3 to 5 minutes. Do not char the dried chilies when toasting them or they will be bitter. Remove the toasted chilies from the pan and set aside.

Pour the peanut or groundnut oil into the same pan and place over medium heat until hot. Carefully drop in the toasted chilies a few at a time, and leave each batch in the oil for a few seconds. The chilies should soften, swell, and smell fragrant, using a slotted utensil, remove the chilies and add them to the toasted sesame seeds. When all of the chilies have been fried, add the bell pepper to the bowl. Reserve the oil, keeping it in the frying pan.

Place the bread and walnuts on a baking sheet in a single layer. Place in the oven until the bread is dry and the walnuts are lightly toasted, 10 to 15 minutes. Stir the walnuts occasionally so they do not burn.

Meanwhile, break the chocolate tablet and cinnamon sticks into 3 or 4 large pieces and place in the bottom of a large bowl. When the toasted walnuts and warm bread are ready, slide them atop the chocolate, to melt it. Set aside.

Reheat the reserved peanut oil in the frying pan over medium heat. When the oil is hot add the whole tomatoes, garlic cloves, tomatillos, plantain/banana chunks, ginger, and onion. Cook until the onion is translucent, the tomatoes begin to char and burst, and the tomatillos have turned a darker green, 7 to 10 mins. Empty the contents into a colander to drain. Discard the oil.

Add the drained vegetable mixture to the large bowl containing the chocolate/bread mixture and stir well. Working in batches, transfer the mixture to a blender, and blend, adding enough water to make the resulting sauce smooth but still thick.

The sauce should have the consistency of a milkshake, but not be as thick as tomato paste. A blender is easier to use than a food processor for this work. Continue to blend in batches until all of the water and the vegetable mixture have been combined. Strain through a mesh strainer or china cap (conically shaped metal strainer), using the back of a wooden spoon to push the purée through.

In a large stockpot, heat the olive oil until it just begins to smoke. Add the puree. This will spit like crazy, so be careful, and take the pan off the flame while adding the purée. Whisk the oil and puree together with a wire whisk until well blended. Turn the heat back on to low and cook, stirring frequently so that the mole does not burn, for 20 minutes.

Taste the mole. If it is too piquant, or bitter, slowly add brown sugar until a balance is achieved between piquant and sweet, if the chilies are quite hot, you may find you have to add quite a lot of sugar! You may also want to add a bit more Mexican chocolate to deepen the flavor. Remove from the heat, but cover to keep hot.

Now instead of cooking a whole chicken, as is the tradition, normally I like to part-poach some chicken breasts and thighs in a saucepan, then finish them off in the mole sauce that slightly less than covers the chicken. You don't want too much sauce. Breasts on their own don't seem to work, it needs a little of the greasiness of the thighs. Girls tend to favor the breasts, so guys, you've got the thighs!

It looks nice if you arrange the chicken pieces in their sauce on a serving plate and sprinkle the remaining toasted sesame seeds over the top, then put it next to the Puerco, the guacamole and the rice and let people serve themselves.

Pollo Mole

INGREDIENTS:

2 chipotle chilies

8 ancho chilies or mulato chilies

8 pasilla negro chilies

1 large red bell pepper

½ cup / 2½ oz / 70g sesame seeds

¾ cup / 6fl oz / 175ml peanut / groundnut oil

¼ loaf French bread, sliced

½ cup walnut pieces (use a tea mug)

½ tablet (1.5 ounces) Mexican chocolate

½ Mexican cinnamon stick

2 Italian plum tomatoes

2 cloves garlic

2 tomatillos, husks removed

1 small plantain or ripe banana, peeled and cut into chunks

1½" piece fresh ginger, sliced in ½" thick rounds

½ large white onion, quartered

8 cups / 2 quarts / 1 ltr water

1 cup / 8fl oz / 250ml olive oil

Approx 1 cup / 8oz / 250g brown sugar, to taste

Part boned chicken breasts and / or chicken thighs

I never had this in a restaurant in New Orleans, however I found it in a recipe book I bought there and as I didn't know many pork recipes, thought I'd try it. It was amazing! I've changed a couple of the ingredients over the years for ones easier to find in the UK, and it was a firm favourite when I was cooking at the N20 restaurant in North London... .

Stuffed Pork Chops

INGREDIENTS:

2 peeled medium apples, coarsely chopped

4, plus 3 tbsps unsalted butter

3 tbsps light brown sugar

1 tsp vanilla extract

1½ tsps ground nutmeg

SEASONING MIX:

1 tbsp salt

1 tsp onion powder

1 tsp ground cayenne pepper

¾ tsp garlic powder

½ tsp white pepper

½ tsp dry mustard

½ tsp rubbed sage

½ tsp ground cumin

½ tsp black pepper

½ tsp dried thyme leaves

6 x 1½ inch-thick pork chops

¾lb/350g minced pork

1 cup chopped onions (use a coffee mug)

1 cup chopped green bell/sweet peppers

2 tsps minced garlic

4oz/100g diced jalapeno chilies and a little of their juice

1 cup/8fl oz/250ml pork or chicken stock

½ cup very fine dry breadcrumbs

½ cup finely chopped large spring/green onions

In a food processor or blender, process the apples, 4 tablespoons of the butter, the sugar, vanilla and nutmeg until smooth, about 3 to 4 minutes. Set aside. In a small bowl thoroughly combine the seasoning mix ingredients; set aside. To prepare the pork chops, there is a small gap just under the fat side and just above the bone. Cut in, using a sharp, long thin knife, and create a pocket inside the chop to hold the stuffing.

In a large frying pan brown the ground pork in the remaining 3 tablespoons butter over high heat for about 3 minutes. Add the onions, bell peppers, garlic and 2 tablespoons of the seasoning mix and stirring well. Cook for about 5 minutes, stirring occasionally and scraping the pan bottom well. Stir in the green chilies and continue cooking until mixture is well browned for about 6 to 8 minutes, stirring occasionally and scraping the pan bottom as needed. Add the stock and cook for 5 minutes, stirring frequently. Stir in the breadcrumbs and cook for about 3 minutes, then add the apple mixture and the green onions. Cook for about 2 minutes more, stirring constantly and scraping the pan bottom as needed. Remove from heat.

Sprinkle the remaining seasoning mix evenly on both sides of the chops, pressing it in by hand. Spoon, and push (!) as much stuffing into each pocket as you can; reserve the remaining stuffing. Place chops on an ungreased baking pan, and bake them at 400ºF/200C/gas mark 6 until meat is done, about 1 hour 10 minutes. Check occasionally, and when the chops are going brown, cover with foil to stop the pork from going dry. Place the remaining stuffing in a small pan in the oven for the last 20 minutes to reheat.

Serve immediately with each chop arranged on top of a portion of the remaining stuffing, sweet potato mash and spinach.

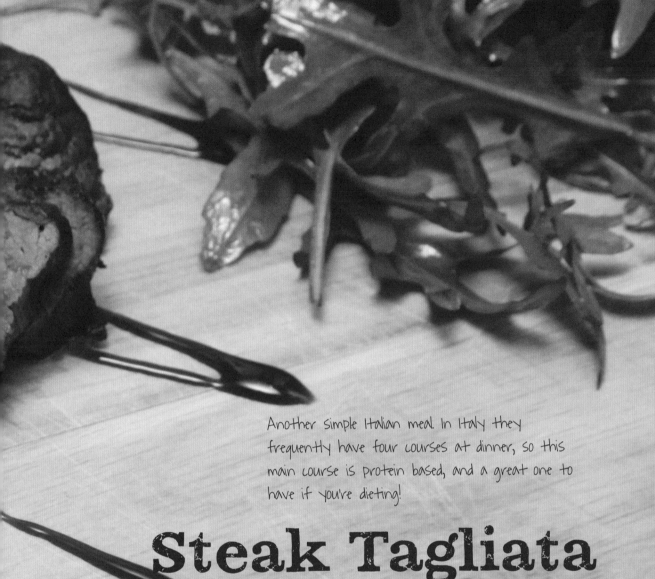

Another simple Italian meal. In Italy they
frequently have four courses at dinner, so this
main course is protein based, and a great one to
have if you're dieting!

Steak Tagliata

INGREDIENTS:

1.35kg/3lb beef fillet

Olive oil

Sea salt

Rough cracked black peppercorns

100g/3½oz rocket leaves

1 tbsp olive oil

One lemon, quartered

Balsamic glaze
(available from most stores)

Cover the beef in clingfilm, and using a tenderizer, beat the
meat down to about 1½"/ 3cm. Brush the steaks with olive
oil and press into the seasoning on both sides. Season with
the salt and black pepper, and press into both sides.

In a ridged frying pan, briskly sear the steaks on one side
until well-browned, then turn once and cook the in same
way for a medium rare result. Set aside to rest.

To serve, with the balsamic glaze make a nice left to right
pattern on a wooden platter. Toss the rocket with the
olive oil and a little of squeezed lemon. Slice the steak into
'fingers', arrange them on a wooden platter, strew with the
lemon quarters, and serve with the rocket.

Oooh, this meat is so lovely and tender that it didn't last long after the photos were taken of this plate... The origins are Mexican, and everybody has their own idea of how it's made, sometimes marinated, sometimes not. But I will say that this marinade, along with how thin you can cut the skirt steak, makes a big difference and puts it above the rest in my view.

Jalapeno chili powder: I'm fast running out and it's hard to find in the UK, so I would double the Chimayo chili powder. See stockists.

In a large glass bowl, stir together the olive oil, Jalapeno and Chimayo chili powders, garlic, salt, red pepper flakes, black pepper, lime juice and onions. Put the steak slices in this mixture and turn them several times to coat well with the marinade. Cover and marinate in the refrigerator for up to 24 hours.

Prepare a fire in a charcoal grill. Criss-cross your grill grates to form a meshed cooking surface, so the grilling foods do not fall through the grate. Alternatively lay a piece of well-perforated aluminium foil across a portion of the grill to act as a guard.

Preheat an oven to 250º F/120ºC/Gas mark ½ . In a dry cast-iron frying pan over high heat, heat the tortillas one at a time, turning once, about 15 secs on each side. Wrap them in a cloth and put in the oven to keep warm.

Remove the meat strips from the marinade and place the meat & onion pieces on the grill rack, only for about 1-2 minutes each side, retaining the moisture of the beef.

You can serve on a plate, with a warm tortilla or two, the tossed salad and the guacamole & the salsa found elsewhere in this book, to eat from the plate or to make a burrito.

INGREDIENTS:

1¼ cups/10fl oz/300g olive oil

2 tbsps plus 2 tsps jalapeno chili powder

2 tbsps Chimayo chili powder

3 tbsps chopped garlic

1 tbsp kosher salt

2 tsps red pepper flakes

1 tsp freshly ground black pepper

2 tbsps fresh lime juice

3 red onions, cut into quarters and separated into pieces

3 pounds beef loin flap (in our case skirt steak), very thinly sliced with the grain and cut into 3 to 5" long pieces

6 to 12 tortillas

3 cups/1½lb/750g guacamole

3 cups/1½lb/750g fresh tomato salsa, (sometimes called Pico de Gallo sauce)

A little mixed leaf salad tossed in olive oil & balsamic

Carne Asada

Try this variation of chile at home:
I've made it a few times and it's
so lovely with guacamole and rice... .
In places like Santa Fe, it's more
of a traditional chile than the
beef one we're used to.

Place the chilies on a baking tray and put into a 250ºF/120ºC/Gas mark
½ oven to toast for 15 mins or so, or toast them in a hot, dry frying pan,
turning them frequently. Remove the stems and seeds and crumble
the rest into a bowl. Cover them with hot water and leave for about
15 mins. Then drain, and discard the water.

Heat the oil in a frying pan on medium heat, add the venison and brown
the meat off. Remove the venison and add the onion; add more oil if
you think it's a little dry, and sauté the onion until it's brown, then add
the garlic and cook for another couple of minutes.

Blend the chilies, onion and garlic together with about ⅓ of the beef
stock until smooth, then push this mixture through a sieve or strainer.

In a large saucepan, combine the chili sauce with the venison and the
remaining stock, bring to the boil, then simmer for about 1-1½ hours,
until the meat is tender and the sauce has thickened.

Venison
Red Chile

INGREDIENTS:

6-8 dried New Mexican chilies

1 ancho chili

1 pasilla chili

2 tbsps vegetable oil

2lb/1kg venison diced into 1½"/4cm cubes

1 large onion, chopped

2 garlic cloves, finely minced

3 cups/750 ml beef stock

Salt to taste

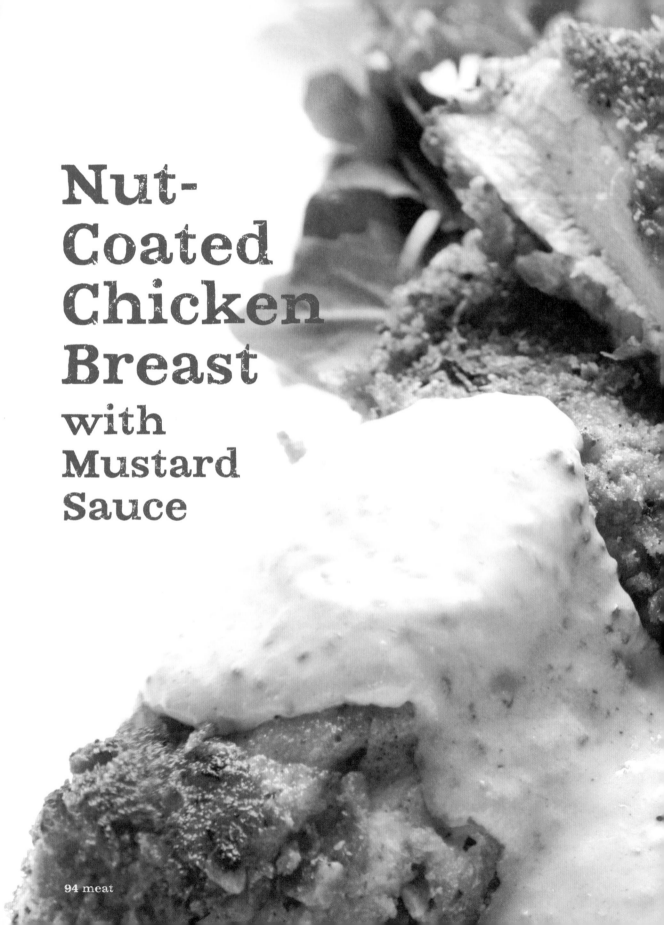

Nut-Coated Chicken Breast
with Mustard Sauce

I had this sauce in New Orleans, but with tenderloin of rabbit. This way you'll probably reach a wider audience, as some folks tend to steer clear of rabbit... .

The idea of coating the chicken breast with nuts came from my music partner back in the 1980s, the Reverend Ian Kewley, in many ways the guy that fired my interest in food.

Nut-Coated Chicken Breast

Combine the nut roast mix, breadcrumbs and the spices into a processor and blitz briefly, so the nuts can still give a bit of crunch to the coating. Beat chicken breasts into escalopes ½ inch thick, dip into the flour, then egg mix and then into the nut seasoning.

In a skillet, heat 1 tablespoon of oil, then add 1 tablespoon butter. Add the chicken breast to the skillet and fry until the nut coating goes a golden brown. Transfer skillet into a 350ºF / 180ºC / gas mark 4 oven to finish off the chicken; warm a portion of mustard sauce through.

To serve, cut the chicken breast in half on the bias, and spoon 2 tablespoons of mustard sauce over the chicken breast. Serve with a salad of mixed leaves, pine nuts, a few cherry tomatoes and an olive oil/lemon dressing.

INGREDIENTS:

½ **cup nut roast mix** (contains peanuts) can be found in most health food shops

½ **cup breadcrumbs**

1 tsp salt

¾ **tsp garlic powder**

½ **tsp onion powder**

¼ **tsp ground cayenne pepper**

¼ **tsp black pepper**

¼ **tsp dried sweet basil leaves**

⅛ **tsp white pepper**

⅛ **tsp ground coriander**

Egg mix

Flour

6 chicken breasts

Olive oil

Unsalted butter

Mustard Sauce

Combine all the ingredients in a small saucepan over medium-low heat. Simmer and stir until thickened, about 15 to 20 minutes, stirring constantly. Cool to room temperature. On its own this sauce has a sour flavour, which is tempered when combined with the chicken.

INGREDIENTS:

½ cup/4fl oz/250ml pouring cream

½ cup/4fl oz/250ml sour cream

6 tbsps wholegrain mustard (preferred) or brown mustard

2 tsps Worcestershire sauce

1½ tsps Dijon mustard

½ tsp salt

¼ tsp black pepper

⅛ tsp white pepper

⅛ tsp ground cayenne pepper

⅛ tsp dried sweet basil leaves

seafood

Blackened Redfish

Fish in Salsa Cabo

Paella

Sea Bream Baked in
a Salt Crust

Portuguese Fish Stew

Pasta con Cozze e Sugo
di Pomodoro

Grilled Squid with Chilies

Barbequed Shrimp
with Basic Cajun Rice

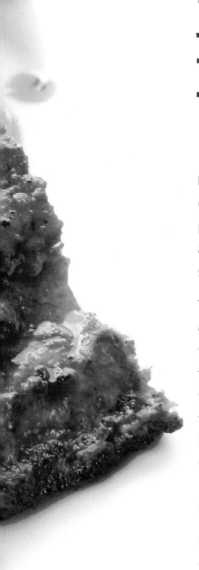

SEASONING MIX:

1 tbsp sweet paprika

1½ tsps salt

1 tsp onion powder

1 tsp garlic powder

1 tsp ground cayenne pepper

¾ tsp white pepper

¾ tsp black pepper

½ tsp dried thyme leaves

½ tsp dried oregano leaves

¾ lb/350g unsalted butter, melted

6 (8-10 oz) fish fillets (preferably redfish, snapper, pompano)

Blackened Redfish

Heat a large cast-iron frying pan over very high heat until it is smoking (the pan cannot be too hot for this dish), at least 10 minutes. Meanwhile, pour 2 tablespoons melted butter in each of 6 small ramekins; set aside and keep warm. Reserve the remaining butter in the frying pan. Heat the serving plates in a 250ºF oven.

Thoroughly combine the seasoning mix ingredients in a small bowl. Dip each fillet in the reserved melted butter so that both sides are well coated; then sprinkle seasoning mix generously and evenly on both sides of the fillets, patting it in by hand. Place in the hot pan skin side up and pour 1 teaspoon melted butter on top of each fillet (be careful, as the butter may flame up). Cook, uncovered, over the same high heat until the underside looks charred, about 2 minutes (the time will vary according to the fillet's thickness and the heat of the skillet). Turn the fish over and again pour 1 teaspoon butter on top; cook until fish is done, about 2 minutes more. Repeat with remaining fillets. Serve each fillet while piping hot.

Place one fillet and a ramekin of butter on each heated plate and serve with a mound of Cajun rice with some lemon basil on top.

I took my wife Stacey for a weekend break in Cabo San Lucas, Mexico, whilst I was song writing in Los Angeles. We didn't take the children, and just as well because there wasn't much for children to do there... in fact, outside the hotel it was fairly under-developed.

So we talked a local fisherman into taking us out on his boat, and then followed him to a restaurant on the edge of the beach where we pleaded with them to feed us, even though they were closed.

The sauce that follows is my best recollection of the simple but wonderful raw sauce they spooned over that recently caught fish!
You can't get fresher than that... .

Fish in Salsa Cabo

Rinse the fish under cold running water to remove any stray scales or traces of blood. Pat dry. Rub the fish inside and out with the chile en adobo, covering everything except the heads. Sprinkle with salt & pepper and refrigerate for about an hour.

To make the sauce, combine the lime juice, coriander, red pepper, chilies and onion in a small bowl. Gradually stir in enough cold water to achieve the texture of a thin sauce. Season with salt and refrigerate while you prepare the fish.

Barbecue as close as possible to the coals, for about 3-4 minutes a side; or you can bake in the fish in a 400ºF/ 200ºC/gas mark 6 oven for about 15 minutes (if they're small).

To serve, fillet the fish and spoon the sauce over the fillets.

INGREDIENTS:

4 small red snappers or sea bass; red mullet is a good locally found fish, cleaned and scaled, heads left on

1 cup chile en adobo (approximately)

Salt and freshly ground white pepper to taste.

For the sauce:

5 tbsps annatto seeds

½ cup/4fl oz/125ml fresh lime juice

A small handful chopped fresh coriander

½ red bell/sweet pepper, de-seeded and chopped

1 fresh chili, jalapeno or serrano, or 2 tbsps jarred jalapenos, chopped

½ small onion, chopped

½ cup/4fl oz/125ml (to taste) cold water

Salt to taste

INGREDIENTS: *Enough for 8-10 people*

1.3 litres/2¼ pints chicken stock

A few strands of saffron

Olive oil

175g/6oz uncooked chorizo, cut in 2.5mm/⅛ in slices

115g/4oz pancetta or smoked streaky bacon cut into strips

8 chicken thighs, chopped in half

1 large onion, finely diced

1 tbsp fresh thyme

2 cloves garlic, roughly chopped

1 tsp dried chili flakes

1 red bell pepper, diced

600g/1¼lb Spanish short-grain paella rice

2 bay leaves

1 tsp paprika

A glass of dry white wine

Juice of half a lemon

115g/4oz frozen peas

10 raw jumbo prawns, in shell

20 mussels, cleaned

55g/2oz unsalted butter

4 tomatoes, de-seeded and diced

4 tbsp flat leaf parsley, chopped

1 lemon, rind only, grated

Salt and freshly ground black pepper

This is such a great traditional Spanish meal. No side dishes of vegetables; it's all-inclusive! Although I like both the seafood and the meat paella, having both all in one meal is the best of both worlds. So I've taken hints from everyone including Spanish family friends about how to make it, and this is the one for me. You have to invest in a large paella pan though!

P.J. Paella

Heat the stock and saffron to boiling point in a saucepan.

Heat 4 tablespoons olive oil in a paella dish or heavy-based saucepan.

Add the chicken and fry for about 5 minutes. Then add the chorizo, pancetta and fry until the chicken skin goes a golden brown. Remove and set aside.

Add another 2 tablespoons olive oil to the pan with the onion, thyme, garlic, the chili flakes and red peppers, and cook over a medium heat for eight minutes or until the onion has softened.

Add the rice, bay leaves and paprika and stir to coat the rice in the oil, cooking and stirring continuously for two minutes.

Stir in the white wine, lemon juice and hot stock and bring to the boil.

Fold in the chorizo, pancetta and browned chicken, along with the peas.

Place the dish, uncovered in a preheated oven (170ºC/325ºF/Gas mark 3) and cook for 15-20 minutes, until the rice is tender and the chicken cooked through.

Remove from the oven and add the prawns and mussels.

Place back in the oven for five minutes until the prawns are cooked and the mussels opened.

Fold in the butter, tomatoes, parsley and grated lemon rind, season to taste with salt and black pepper and serve.

Sea Bream Baked in a Salt Crust

This reminds me of the best time I had this dish, in Sardinia at a harbour restaurant... show off! At the time, I had one of those stop-still moments when you think, does life get any better than this?

It really is one of those meals that tastes so refined, decadent and yet downright healthy. The salt crust holds in the flavour of the fish so well!

If you make this for your friends, they will think you're a master chef, but believe me, it's got to be about the easiest of all the fish recipes. Just ask your fishmonger to scale and gut the fish for you, the rest is straightforward.

The only difficult part is to get the delicate flesh off the bone and onto the plate, but I've never seen any waiter get the whole fillet plated in one go, so it doesn't really matter; you'll get better with practise anyway.

Sea Bream Baked in a Salt Crust

Preheat your oven to 200°C/400°F/Gas Mark 6. In a mixing bowl, mix the rock salt with the 2 eggs, which will bind the salt around the fish. Lay a large piece of tin foil (about 3" over both the head and tail, and enough to wrap comfortably around the fish) on your worktop. Season the inside of the fish with salt & pepper.

Spoon a reasonable amount of the salt/egg mixture onto the foil and lay the fish on top. Crunch up the foil around the head & tail, and create a kind of open pitta bread effect at the top, to which you spoon in enough salt to comfortably cover the fish. Close the top of the foil snugly around your first fish and then repeat with the second.

Place on a baking sheet or tin, and bake in the oven for about 45 minutes.

Remove from the oven, open the foil and carefully crack the salt with the blunt side, or handle of your knife, and brush the salt to one side. Make one incision just behind the head, and another close to the tail. Then carefully make an incision along, but slightly to one side of the backbone. The skin should peel away quite nicely. Then using your fattest knife, lift as much flesh as you can onto the blade and transfer it to a warm plate.

When you've removed as much flesh as you can, lift out the skeleton of the fish to reach the other fillet.

Drizzle with extra virgin olive oil and lemon juice, and a little fresh black pepper. Serve with some delicate veg, like steamed baby corn and snap peas, tossed in a little butter. Or with a salad and I'm back in Sardinia.... .

INGREDIENTS:

2 sea bream

4lb/2kg rock salt

2 eggs

Extra virgin olive oil

Lemons

Salt & pepper

A lovely Mediterranean stew; serve yourself a glass of white wine with this and fool yourself you're looking over the sea somewhere in the Med... .

Portuguese Fish Stew

INGREDIENTS:

2 x 2 tbsps olive oil

One thinly sliced onion

2 cloves garlic

A handful of fresh chopped thyme

½ tsp chili flakes, or one small green chili, chopped & de-seeded

Pinch of saffron

One large glass of white wine

One fish stock cube

One jar of passata + half that quantity of water

Juice of half a lemon

450g/1lb new potatoes, pre-roasted

2 fillets monkfish, chopped into 2 inch pieces

1 dozen mussels, raw

1 dozen shrimp, raw

2 medium squid; slice the heads

A fistful chopped parsley

First of all, pre-heat your oven to 180ºC/350ºF, gas mark 4. Pour a couple of tablespoons of olive oil or goose fat into a baking dish and toss the new potatoes in the oil.

Roast the potatoes in the oven, about 45 minutes (check to see if they are a golden brown), then remove.

Heat 2 tablespoons olive oil in a large pot.

Add sliced onions, garlic, one small handful chopped fresh thyme, the chili and a pinch of saffron.

When softened add the white wine and a fish, or veg stock cube (I sometimes add a tin of lobster bisque for more flavour) and cook until the alcohol smell has gone.

Add a jar of passata and half that quantity of water. Simmer for an hour.

Season to taste and add juice of half of a lemon.

Add your pre-roasted new potatoes, then add the chopped monkfish.

After a couple of minutes add the mussels.

After a couple of minutes add the prawns.

The same with the sliced squid.

Add your chopped parsley.

Serve with griddled ciabatta, and a topping of breadcrumbs, lemon zest and more chopped parsley.

INGREDIENTS:

Dried spaghetti

1kg / 2lb mussels in their shells

4 tbsps of olive oil

2 cloves of garlic

2 x 400g / 14oz cans of chopped tomatoes

Sea salt, black pepper

Fresh parsley

The first time I had mussels it was in the well-known French style, with a white wine and cream sauce, garlic and lots of French loaf. I prefer however, this more Italian style with pasta and tomatoes, much more hearty. I sometimes add half a teaspoon of chili flakes or one fresh chopped chili in with the garlic just to liven it up a little, especially in the winter.

Rope-grown mussels are easy to find in supermarkets these days, and need less cleaning! But always check for any open shells first: tap them on the side of the sink, and if they close they're fine. After they're cooked, it's the reverse; if they're closed, don't eat 'em!

Pasta con Cozze e Sugo di Pomodoro

First, put a big pan of water on, generously salted, to boil (for the pasta) while we prepare the mussels.

Clean the mussels under cold water, pulling the 'beards' away from the shells. Put them into a big saucepan on the heat, cover them and let them steam for 4-5 minutes turning them occasionally. Remove from the heat, take out the mussels and put them to one side. Strain the liquid through a fine sieve, then put that mussel water back on the heat to reduce it while you make the tomato sauce.

In a frying pan, heat the olive oil and add the garlic: you can finely chop it if you like. I sometimes just take the skin off them and crush them slightly under my knife then put them in the oil. My wife has migraine problems and garlic doesn't help, but if I put them in whole then remove them at the end, it seems to help. Don't ask me why!

Add the tomatoes, and while they're heating crush them a little with a potato masher. I don't like the sauce to be too smooth, like passata, so this is a better way to have a hearty sauce. On medium heat, reduce the sauce for about 15-20 minutes, and add the mussel liquid once it has reduced to about 3 dessertspoonfuls.

While the sauce is cooking, put enough spaghetti for 4 into your boiling salted water. Tip: next time you buy spaghetti, pinch a strand of spaghetti through the plastic wrapping and run your fingernails down. If it's smooth, don't buy it; get the spaghetti that feels rougher. That way the sauce sticks better to the cooked spaghetti. Cook for the amount suggested on the packet, in fact try it a couple of minutes before just to get it on the very edge of cooked. Over-cooked pasta is very limp and not a nice texture.

Add the mussels in their shells to the sauce before you drain the pasta, to give them a chance to warm through. Put the spaghetti into a big serving bowl, pour the mussels and tomato over the pasta, toss a handful of freshly chopped parsley over the top and put that in the middle of the table with a big serving spoon: dig in!

Grilled Squid with Chilies

Clean the squid by cutting the body open to make a flat piece. Scrape out the guts, keeping the tentacles in their bunches but removing the eyes and mouth.

Using a serrated knife, score the inner side of the flattened squid body with parallel lines 1cm (½ inch) apart, and then equally apart the other way to make cross-hatching.

Put the chopped chili in a bowl and cover with about 2.5cm (1inch) of the oil. Season with salt & pepper.

Place the squid (including the tentacles) scored side down on a very hot grill, season with salt & pepper and grill for 1-2 minutes. Turn the squid pieces over; they will immediately curl up, by which time they will be cooked.

To make the oil & lemon dressing, whisk together 6 tablespoons of extra virgin olive oil with about 2 tablespoons of lemon juice, and season with salt & pepper. Toss the rocket in the dressing. Arrange a squid body and tentacles on each plate with some of the rocket. Place a little of the chili on the squid and serve with lemon quarters.

INGREDIENTS: *Serves 6*

6 medium squid, about the size of your hand. *You can ask your fishmonger to clean them for you.*

10 fresh red chilies, seeded and finely chopped

Extra virgin olive oil

Sea salt and freshly ground black pepper

8 tbsps oil and lemon dressing

225g/8 oz rocket leaves

3 lemons

Barbequed Shrimp

Barbecued shrimp: a strange title, since these are neither barbequed, nor are they what we call shrimp! We think of the tiny shrimp we get in a shrimp cocktail, but in New Orleans these giant Tiger shrimp are used in many dishes. I imagined that the beer should be a lager-based beer, not as overpowering as a more typical British beer.

Also, even though this is essentially a Creole recipe, I think it goes great with that heavenly Mexican invention, guacamole. You will find my favourite version of this (and there are many different variations of guacamole) elsewhere in this book.

Barbequed Shrimp

While rinsing the shrimp in cold water, pinch off and discard the portion of the head from the eyes forward (including the eyes, but not the protruding long spine above the eyes). Leave as much as possible of the orange shrimp fat from the head attached to the body. Set aside to drain.

In a small bowl or ramekin combine the seasoning mix ingredients. Combine ¼ lb/100g of the butter, the garlic, Worcestershire and seasoning mix in a large frying pan over high heat. When the butter is melted, add the shrimp. Cook for 2 minutes, shaking the pan as opposed to stirring. You can turn the shrimp if you want to get the toasty effect on both sides. Add the remaining 5 tablespoons butter and the stock; cook and shake pan for 2 minutes. Add the beer and cook and shake the pan 1 minute longer. Remove from heat.

Arrange the shrimp on to four warm plates, then go back to the sauce in the frying pan. Mix half a teaspoon of cornflour with a little cold water and add to the sauce, whisking all the time until thickened. If you feel it's still a little runny, repeat the process. This sauce is wonderful once it's seeped into the rice, and very more-ish even after the shrimp have gone!

This looks nice served with cooked rice mounded in the middle and the shrimp and sauce surrounding it, with a bowl of guacamole on the side; or if you prefer, forget the rice and serve with a warm French loaf to dip in the sauce.

INGREDIENTS: *Servings 4*

2 dozen large Tiger shrimp with heads and shells (about 1 lb/500g)

¼ lb/100g plus 5 tbsps unsalted butter

1½ tsps minced garlic

1 tsp Worcestershire sauce

½ cup/4fl oz/125g shrimp or fish stock

¼ cup/2fl oz/60g beer at room temperature

½ tsp cornflour

SEASONING MIX:

½ tsp ground cayenne pepper

½ tsp black pepper

½ tsp salt

½ tsp crushed red pepper

½ tsp dried thyme leaves

½ tsp dried rosemary leaves, crushed

The great thing about baking rice is that once you've set the oven timer, you can forget about it and get on with the other parts of the meal, which usually takes a little more or less than an hour with the prep and the cooking! Perfect... Use whatever stock suits your meal, although I favour the chicken stock... .

Basic Cajun Rice

In a 5x9x2½ inch loaf pan, combine all ingredients; mix well. Seal pan snugly with aluminium foil. Bake at 350F/180C/Gas Mark 4 in the middle of the oven until the rice is tender, about 1 hour, 10 minutes. Serve immediately. However, you can count on the rice staying hot for 45 minutes and warm for 2 hours.

INGREDIENTS: *Enough for 6 people*

2 cups/16oz/500g long grain rice

2½ cups/1¼ pints/750ml chicken stock

1½ tbsps very finely chopped onion

1½ tbsps very finely chopped celery

1½ tbsps of each finely chopped green, red & yellow sweet peppers

1½ tbsps unsalted butter (preferred), melted

½ tsp salt

⅛ tsp garlic powder

A pinch each of white pepper, ground red pepper (preferably cayenne) and black pepper

1 tsp vanilla extract

desserts

Lemon Tart

Bramley Apple Crumble

Sweet Potato Pecan Pie

Strawberry Pie

New Orleans Bread Pudding
with Lemon Sauce

A lemon tart is very sophisticated to most guests, yet it's deceptively easy and delicious if you follow these guidelines... .

I love lemon tart as a dessert. And as an afternoon treat with an espresso it's delectable!

Lemon Tart

Preheat the oven to 160ºC / 325ºF / Gas mark 4.

Put all the ingredients except the butter in a large saucepan over a very low heat, and whisk until the eggs have broken up and the sugar has dissolved.

Add half the butter and continue to whisk. At this point the eggs will start to cook and the mixture will coat the back of a spoon. Add the remaining butter and continue stirring until the mixture becomes very thick. It is important to continue whisking throughout the cooking process to prevent the mixture from curdling. Remove from the heat, place on a cold surface and continue to whisk until lukewarm.

Raise the oven temperature to 230ºC / 450ºF / Gas mark 8.

Spoon the lemon filling into the pastry bases and bake until the top is brown, about 5-8 minutes.

INGREDIENTS:

2 pastry cases (yes; pastry is a knack, so either practise or cheat!)

Finely grated zest and juice of 7 lemons

350g/12oz/1¼ cups caster sugar

6 whole eggs

9 egg yolks

300g/10oz unsalted butter, softened

During the late 90s, we lived in an old split mansion near Hereford. Our neighbours, who lived in a cottage in the same grounds, had a beautiful apple orchard and would give us a generous supply, hence the reason for including this tempting English favourite! You will need baking beans to put in the uncooked pastry case, available from most large supermarkets.

Bramley Apple Crumble

INGREDIENTS:

For the pastry:

185g/6½oz unsalted butter

225g/8oz caster sugar

3 medium egg yolks

300g/10½oz plain flour

For the apple filling:

55g/2oz unsalted butter

6 large Bramleys, peeled, cored and roughly chopped

140g/5oz caster sugar

For the crumble topping:

100g/3½oz unsalted butter, finely diced

55g/2oz ground almonds

110g/4oz caster sugar

150g/5½oz plain flour

To serve, Cornish clotted cream

First make the pastry. In a food processor, mixer or by hand, cream the butter and icing sugar together until smooth. Add the egg yolks, mix well, then fold in the flour. Press the dough into a ball and refrigerate it for a couple of hours. Or, buy ready-to-use pastry!

To assemble, grease a 25-cm tart tin. Roll the pastry on a floured table to 5 mm thick. Line the tin with the pastry, trim the edges and refrigerate for 2-3 hours.

Meanwhile, for the filling, melt the butter in a pan, put in the apples and cook them until they are soft. Remove them from the heat and stir in the sugar. Put all the crumble ingredients in a food processor or mixer and process until they look like breadcrumbs.

Pre-heat the oven to 175ºC/gas mark 4. Line the pastry case with a sheet of clingfilm, pour in your baking beans and bake blind for 10-15 minutes until the pastry is light golden. Remove the beans and the clingfilm and fill the pastry case with the warm apple mixture. Sprinkle the crumble over the top and bake for 20-30 minutes until the top is golden brown.

Serve with a generous spoonful of lovely Cornish clotted cream.

This is a traditional New Orleans dessert; in the UK we are used to finding pecan tart in coffee shops as a snack. This is a much more hearty pie, and the addition of the sweet potato actually stops it from being too sweet & sickly.

You could also reduce the sugar quantities a little if you don't have such a sweet tooth!

Sweet Potato Pecan Pie

You will need an 8 inch deep pan dish (about 1½ inch high) for the pastry, and unfortunately most pre-made pie cases in the supermarkets are too shallow, so the next easiest option is to buy the fresh rolled dough and bake the casing yourself. Pour some rice into the pie shell to stop it from rising and 'blind bake' it in a 350F / 180C / Gas mark 4 oven for 15 minutes. Let it cool before adding the filling.

For the sweet-potato filling: Combine all the ingredients in a mixing bowl. Beat on medium speed of electric mixer until the batter is smooth, about 2 to 3 minutes should be enough.

For the pecan pie syrup: Combine all the ingredients except the pecans in a mixing bowl. Mix thoroughly on slow speed of electric mixer until the syrup is opaque, about 1 minute; stir in pecans and set aside.

To assemble: Spoon the sweet potato filling evenly into the dough-lined cake pan. Pour the pecan syrup on top. Bake in a 325F/160C/Gas mark 3 oven until a knife inserted in the center comes out clean, about 1¾ hours.

Cool and serve with double cream. Store pie at room temperature for the first 24 hours, then if there is any left, refrigerate.

INGREDIENTS: *Makes one 8 inch pie*

Sweet potato filling:

2 to 3 sweet potatoes (or enough to yield 1 cup cooked pulp), baked preferably, or boiled and mashed

¼ cup / 2oz / 55g packed, light brown sugar

2 tbsps sugar

½ egg, vigorously beaten until frothy

1 tbsp single cream

1 tbsp unsalted butter, softened

1 tbsp vanilla extract

¼ tsp salt

¼ tsp ground cinnamon

⅛ tsp ground allspice

⅛ tsp ground nutmeg

Pecan pie syrup:

¾ cup / 6oz / 170g sugar

¾ cup / 6fl oz / 175ml dark corn syrup

2 small eggs

1½ tbsps unsalted butter, melted

2 tsps vanilla extract

Pinch of salt

Pinch of ground cinnamon

¾ cup pecan pieces

This is nothing but strawberries; even the gelatin is mixed with strawberries and as such is a pure taste, unlike the ones with the custard base that are served in tea and coffee shops.

Strawberry Pie

You will need an 1.5 inch deep pan dish for the pastry, and unfortunately most pre-made pie cases in the supermarkets are too shallow, so the next easiest option is to buy the fresh rolled dough and bake the casing yourself. Pour some rice into the pie shell to stop it from rising and 'blind bake' it in a 350F / 180C / Gas mark 4 oven for 15 minutes. Let it cool before adding the filling.

Clip any green tips from the strawberries. Arrange the strawberries in the cooked pie crusts, stem ends down and in circles with the largest berries in the centre. Then use smaller berries and for the outer circle cut berries in half lengthwise and arrange cut side down with tips pointing outward. (I sometimes trim the larger ones down from the stem end, so they are of a more uniform height, then use the trimmed pieces alongside the remaining strawberries to make the gelatin mixture.) Refrigerate for 30 minutes.

Place 6 cups / 1½ quarts / 1.75 ltrs of the remaining strawberries, and the sugar in a food processor or blender; process until smooth, about 10 to 20 seconds. Transfer mixture to a large saucepan. Add the water. Bring to a boil over high heat and boil for about 3 minutes, stirring occasionally. Remove from heat and pour into a large bowl. Add the gelatin and beat with a metal whisk until gelatin is dissolved. Set aside to cool.

Ladle half the strawberry sauce over the top of each pie, coating all the berries well. Refrigerate for at least 2 hours (until sauce is firm) before serving. If you wish you may serve the pie with Chantilly cream.

INGREDIENTS: *Makes two 9 inch pies*

6 lbs / 2.7kg strawberries, in all, rinsed
and stems removed

1 cup / 8oz / 250g sugar

½ cup / 4fl oz / 120ml water

2 envelopes unflavoured gelatin

New Orleans Bread Pudding
served with Lemon Sauce

Absolutely yummy: New Orleans food can sometimes have a close association with British food, hence this variation on our own bread pudding. Serve it this way for a welcome surprise for your guests.

New Orleans Bread Pudding

With an electric mixer, beat the eggs on high speed until frothy and bubbly, about 3 minutes. Add the sugar, vanilla, nutmeg, cinnamon and butter and beat on high until well blended. Beat in the milk, then stir in the raisins and pecans.

Place the bread cubes in a greased loaf pan. Pour the egg mixture over them and toss until the bread is soaked. Let it sit until you see only a narrow film of liquid around the pan's edges, about 45 minutes, and pat the bread down into the liquid occasionally. If you feel it's still too dry, add a little more milk. Place in a pre-heated 350ºF/180ºC/gas mark 4 oven. Immediately lower the heat to 300ºF/150ºC/gas mark 2 and bake for 40 minutes. Increase oven temperature to 425ºF/220ºC/gas mark 7 and bake until pudding is well browned and puffy, about 15 to 20 minutes more.

To serve, put a wedge of hot bread pudding in a bowl, spoon some warm lemon sauce over it and top with a (not-so) healthy dessert spoonful of lovely Cornish clotted cream!

INGREDIENTS:

3 large eggs

1¼ cups/10oz/300g sugar

1½ tsps vanilla extract

1¼ tsps ground nutmeg

1¼ tsps ground cinnamon

¼ cup/2oz/50g unsalted butter, melted

2 cups/1 pint/600ml milk

½ cup raisins*

½ cup coarsely chopped pecans, dry roasted*

5 cups very stale French or Italian bread cubes, with crusts on*

* Note: An American 'cup' is what we English call a mug: so it's easier, rather than talking weight, to measure the raisins, pecans and bread in this way.

This sauce accompanies the New Orleans Bread & Butter Pudding: a kind of home-cooking way of making a beautiful sauce!

Lemon Sauce

Squeeze 2 tablespoons juice from the lemon halves and place juice in a small saucepan; add the lemon halves, water and sugar and bring to a boil.
Stir in the dissolved cornstarch and vanilla. Cook 1 minute over high heat, stirring constantly. Strain, squeezing the sauce from the lemon rinds. Makes about ¾ cup. Serve warm.

INGREDIENTS:

1 lemon, halved

½ cup/4fl oz/125ml water

¼ cup/2oz/60g sugar

2 tsps cornstarch dissolved in ¼ cup / 2fl oz / 60ml water

1 tsp vanilla extract

side dishes

Fresh Tomato Salsa

Guacamole

Chimayo Chile &
Bacon Corn Muffins

Black Beans

Saffron Rice

Creole Vegetable Hash

Chargrilled Vegetables

Fresh Tomato Salsa

Here's my favourite tomato salsa: it goes hand in hand with the guacamole recipe I chose because, if you're going to add coriander to your salsa, don't put it in the guacamole! Separate the flavours... .

INGREDIENTS:

10 ounces / 280 g Italian plum tomatoes (about 5)

¼ white onion

½ fresh serrano chili or 1 fresh jalapeno chili, stemmed, seeded, and finely minced

¼ cup fresh coriander leaves & some stems, chopped

¼ tsp salt (roughly)

A small pinch of ground cumin

Chop the tomatoes by hand. To create a perfect ⅛ inch dice, slice off the stem end and stand the tomato on its now flat surface. Slice straight down to make ⅛ inch-wide slabs. Turn the tomato on its side, keeping the slices together and removing one side piece to make a flat surface. Cut ⅛ inch lengths, creating strips. Turn the cut tomato as a unit and cut across the tomato in ⅛ inch increments, creating a dice. Cut the reserved slice into dice as well. Put the diced tomatoes into a non-reactive bowl.

Cut the onion in the same size dice as the tomatoes and put in the bowl with the tomatoes. Add the chili and coriander. Add the salt and a very small amount of cumin. Stir well.

Note: Serve the salsa at room temperature within a few hours of preparing. It does not store well; the tomatoes and onion become broken down by the salt and the flavours dissipate.

My daughter Levi calls this 'the world's greatest invention', as when you get the mix right: the texture, the fruity chili flavour of the serrano chili or jalapeno and the sharpness of the lemons, it's a seductive combination!

Serrano chilies are hard to find in the UK, but jalapenos are a worthy substitute.

You will find many different versions of guacamole; I have a great book at home that shows regional Mexican recipes, and guacamole varies from region to region. But this one is the one I arrived at as being my favourite. Once you've had this rough mashed version you'll never buy that blended processed guacamole again... .

Guacamole

The easiest way to dice an avocado: slice in half, and the stone will stay in one side. Using your sharp knife, be brave and hack into the side of the stone. The stone should lift out of the half avocado (depending on how ripe your avocados are) then just scrape the flat side of the knife on the side of your bin and the stone should fall neatly into your bin. Clean the knife! Then make gentle criss-cross patterns in the flesh, taking care not to cut through the skin. Using a teaspoon, spoon the flesh into your mixing bowl. Done! Mash roughly with a fork.

De-seed the tomato by slicing the head of the tomato off (stalk end). Stand on its end and slice into quarters. It should be easy now to slice the seeds and the pithy stuff away from the skin & flesh. Dice the tomato and add to the avocados.

Add the diced onion, the chili (deseeded as well, unless it's pickled) and the finely chopped garlic, and fold into the mixture. Lastly, season with salt & pepper and add the juice of one lemon and taste. There is a balance between the salt and the lemon that is historic in Mexican cuisine (if you've had tequila, salt and lemon; you'll know what I mean) and should become apparent the more you make this. If you feel it needs it, add a little more lemon juice. I definitely think lemon is better than lime in guacamole.

INGREDIENTS:

3 large ripe avocados

1 tomato

½ small white onion, diced finely

1 serrano chili, or jalapeno

1 clove garlic (optional)

Salt & black pepper

Juice of 1-2 lemons

Southwestern cuisine is a great fusion of influences from the south of the USA, where the borders meet. You've got the traditional American cooking fusing with Mexican, Asian and Caribbean... These muffins, a Mexican twist on a U.S. favourite, are great alongside the Mexican breakfast, Huevos Rancheros.

Chimayo Chile & Bacon Corn Muffins

Preheat the oven to 425ºF/220ºC/gas mark 7.

Fry the bacon in a skillet until it's crisp. Remove the bacon, drain it on a paper towel, and crumble it, or slice thinly with scissors. Reserve the drippings to add more flavour to the mix.

In a large mixing bowl, sift together the cornmeal, flour, sugar, baking powder, chile and salt. Set the mixture aside. In another bowl, combine the milk, egg, butter or drippings and bacon. Add the liquid to the dry ingredients and stir to just mix them.

Lightly oil a muffin pan and divide the batter evenly among 12 to 15 muffin cups, filling up each one about halfway. Bake for 15 to 20 minutes.

Cool the muffins on a rack and serve them warm or at room temperature. Makes 12 to 15 muffins.

INGREDIENTS:

4-5 strips bacon

¼ cup/2oz/50g blue cornmeal

1 cup/5oz/150g plain flour

1/3 cup/3oz/80g sugar

3 tsps baking powder

1 tsp ground red chimayo chile

¾ tsp salt

1 cup/8fl oz/250ml milk

1 egg, beaten

2 tbsps melted butter, or bacon drippings

The food in Mexico was mainly vegetarian, until the Spanish introduced meat into their diet. They were big on corn and beans, great for me because I love them both.

Black beans are possibly my favourite, the meatiest of the bunch, and although I also love black bean soup, this time around I'll include this great accompaniment to most of the Mexican dishes you find in this book. Most recipes seem to require soaking of the beans overnight, but I found when I did it this way, the beans were just as nice, in fact maybe a bit softer. Also, just like soups, cooked beans seem to improve when frozen, so make more than enough and freeze them in small containers to be de-frosted as and when...

Also, re-frying them in goose fat isn't necessary, you could use vegetable oil; but if you're not vegetarian it's a way of adding that little something to the already meaty flavour of the beans.

Black Beans

Most supermarket dried beans are pre-sorted and cleaned, but it's still worth sorting for any small rocks and debris, even though I don't think you'll find any! Then rinse them off and add to a big pot with all the ingredients except the salt and goose fat.

Bring to the boil and then simmer uncovered for about 1½ hrs. Keep an eye on the water and add more, to keep the beans immersed. Once soft, add salt to taste and let them cool.

I like to take about ¼ to ⅓ of the beans and blend them, or even better in a food processor, before stirring them back into the pot to thicken the liquid into a sauce.

Then, when you're ready to use them, add a couple of tablespoons of goose fat to a frying pan, add a cup of beans in their juice and bring to the boil. Reduce on medium high heat until the liquid is the consistency of olive oil, and serve, with the Huevos Rancheros, Puerco Pibil, or whatever takes your fancy.

INGREDIENTS:

1¼ lbs/2½ cups dried black beans

½ white onion, diced

½ red pepper, seeded, de-veined and diced

2 fresh jalapenos, stemmed seeded and diced, or 2 tbsps jarred chilies, chopped

½ tsp ground cumin

1 bay leaf

2 ¾ l of water

1 tsp salt approx

Goose fat

Saffron Rice

Toast the saffron in a small frying pan, over a medium heat, shaking it to stop the strands from burning, for about two minutes. Remove from the pan and let cool.

In a large saucepan on a medium heat, add the oil, then the onion, garlic, salt & pepper. Stir around for a couple of minutes until all the rice is coated and the pan is going dry, then add 3 cups (750ml) of water, stir in the saffron and bring to the boil.

Reduce the heat to a simmer, put the saucepan lid on and leave until all the water is absorbed, that's around 20-30 minutes.

INGREDIENTS: *Serves 4-6*

1 tsp saffron strands

¼ cup/60ml/2 fl oz olive oil

½ white onion, very finely chopped

2 tsps finely chopped garlic

1½ tsps salt

½ tsp white pepper

2 cups/480g/1lb 2oz long grain rice

This is an interesting way of doing a vegetable dish, which can be either a side accompaniment, or a vegetarian meal in itself, either on it's own or over pasta

Creole Vegetable Hash

Combine the seasoning, mix ingredients in a ramekin.

Melt 2 tablespoons of the butter with the olive oil in a large frying pan or 5-quart pot, preferably non-stick, over high heat. As soon as the butter begins to sizzle, add all the vegetables, the garlic, and the seasoning mix. Stir well, then cover and cook, uncovering to stir and scrape the bottom of the pan frequently, for 8 minutes. Now the fennel will be wilted, transparent, and tender and the bottom of the pan will be dry. At this point the vegetables are partially cooked but still retain some of their crunch.

At this point add the chopped tomatoes, stir, re-cover and cook, uncovering every 2 or 3 minutes: to stir, scrape, and check to be sure the mixture is not going to scorch… just until the liquid has evaporated, about another 8 minutes. If you feel that there might be a risk of over browning, then reduce the heat slightly. Add the stock, brown sugar, and the remaining 2 tablespoons butter. This red sauce will now have a slightly sweeter taste that balances the acidity of the tomatoes. Stir well until the butter is thoroughly melted into the sauce and the vegetables are tender, except for the celery, which should still be crunchy, about 2-3 minutes. Serve as an accompaniment to your Cajun dishes, or even serve hot over pasta.

SEASONING MIX:

1 ½ tsps salt

1 ¼ tsps ground cardamom

1 ¼ tsps cayenne pepper

1 ¼ tsps onion powder

1 tsp ground cumin

¾ tsp garlic powder

¾ tsp dry mustard

½ tsp dried oregano

½ tsp dried thyme leaves

¼ tsp ground allspice

¼ tsp white pepper

INGREDIENTS:

4 tbsps unsalted butter, in all

2 tbsps olive oil

1½ cups (approx 3 medium) onions cut into ½ inch pieces

1 cup (approx one whole) seeded red peppers cut into ½ inch pieces

1 cup seeded yellow peppers cut into ½ inch pieces

1 cup seeded green peppers cut into ½ inch pieces

1½ cups (approx 2 large) parsnips, peeled and cut into ½ inch pieces

3 cups (approx 1 small-size) butternut squash, cut into ½ inch pieces

1½ cups or 5 stalks celery, cut into ½ inch pieces

1 fennel bulb, cut into ½ inch pieces (about 2 cups)

1 tbsp minced fresh garlic

1 x 14oz tin chopped tomatoes

1 cup/8 fl oz/250ml vegetable stock

1 tbsp lightly packed dark brown sugar

More often than not, you'll find lots of main course ideas in recipe books, but then I'm stuck as to what to do vegetable wise; this idea goes not with just some of the Mexican recipes found here, but also as they are best barbequed (I don't have an indoor grill), serve on a hot summer's day with whatever else you're grilling... .

Chargrilled Vegetables

Put the vegetables into a sealable bag, and pour the mixed marinade over the top. Seal the bag, shake to coat the vegetables in the marinade and leave at room temperature for a few hours. Every so often roll the bag to make sure the vegetables are evenly coated.

When the barbeque is ready, place the vegetables on the hot grill and turn frequently until they're charred, for about 7-12 minutes depending on the heat of the grill.

FOR THE MARINADE:
250ml/1 cup olive oil
90ml/1/3 cup balsamic vinegar
1 tbsp minced garlic
Salt & fresh ground black pepper

VEGETABLES:
1 large red onion, sliced into thick wedges
2 red peppers, seeded and cut into 1"/1 cm slices
2 yellow squash (if you can find them), cut lengthwise into ½ cm/¼" strips
2 courgettes, sliced lengthwise into ½ cm/¼" strips
2 aubergines, sliced lengthwise into ½ cm/¼" strips
A bunch or two of large spring onions (scallions), trimmed at the top

DESDE
1943

TEQUILA

Sombrero

100%

PURO DE AGAVE

Ah, Tequila!
my personal favourite tipple...

Some people have too much of this once and can't drink or even smell it again without feeling nauseous. For me, that is true of Southern Comfort, but tequila? It is my friend; I have always had a great night on this, because I know when to stop.

TEQUILA

I remember in the early 80s I was at a record company convention in Cornwall, and the last stragglers repaired to the bar, where I suggested a round of tequilas. Once we started, it was like reflex action: "and another!" someone always said. However, I know when to cut out, and once I'd started the action, I got out while the going was good... .

Over breakfast, I heard of one record company guy who had stripped off and gone for a swim in the algae-riddled outside swimming pool at 3 in the morning; in November!! Tequila does that... . But I'm not here to talk about that side of tequila.

In the 90s I discovered the more refined tequila; the real tequila, not the cheaply mass-produced stuff that is slugged with salt & lemon, but the tequila that is sipped from a small glass, and should be seen more like a fine blend scotch.

It became the "It" drink in Los Angeles in the late 80s with all the Leonardo/Johnny Depp/River Phoenix set, and now it seems to sit just as comfortably with the glitterati as with the farmers that made it originally.

A little history: the art of making tequila is taken seriously by the Mexican government; in fact some people joke that if they were as rigid with their other laws, the streets would be wiped clean of all degenerates and drug dealing!

Tequila is made from the Blue Agave plant (which isn't actually a cactus), which must only be grown in Jalisco and a few designated areas in four other states. Anything less than 100% Blue Agave is called a "mixto", and the 100% bottles must be marked as such to show that they are the highest quality.

The Mexican government actually owns the moniker "Tequila"! Note: these 100% tequilas contain some of the lowest amounts of hangover-inducing methanol of any alcohol, so don't blame the tequila... and while we're on it, some doctors say a glass of tequila can lower your cholesterol... .

For me, I prefer the silver tequilas (sounds great too); the gold tequilas are only so because of the addition of caramel, or molasses. The word 'reposado', or rested, is worth looking for on the bottle as it means it has been aged in oak casks for a few months; and "añejo" means that it has been aged for a year or more.

Over here in the UK, your usual bottle of tequila will retail for about £17 per 70cl. When you're looking at a price tag of around £40 (and they can stretch to about £400 a bottle), then you're in the big league. Patron is one of the leading fine tequila makers; others like Perfidio and Herradura have found their way onto, and off my shelves! So get your local off-licence to order some exotic brands, and enjoy the taste of Mexico.

Paul at Number 6 Restaurant,
Padstow with owner Paul Ainsworth

Paul and Simon Stallard
of The Hidden Hut cooking
outdoors at The Lost
Gardens of Heligan, Cornwall.

Paul opening Cornwall Food & Drink Festival, Truro

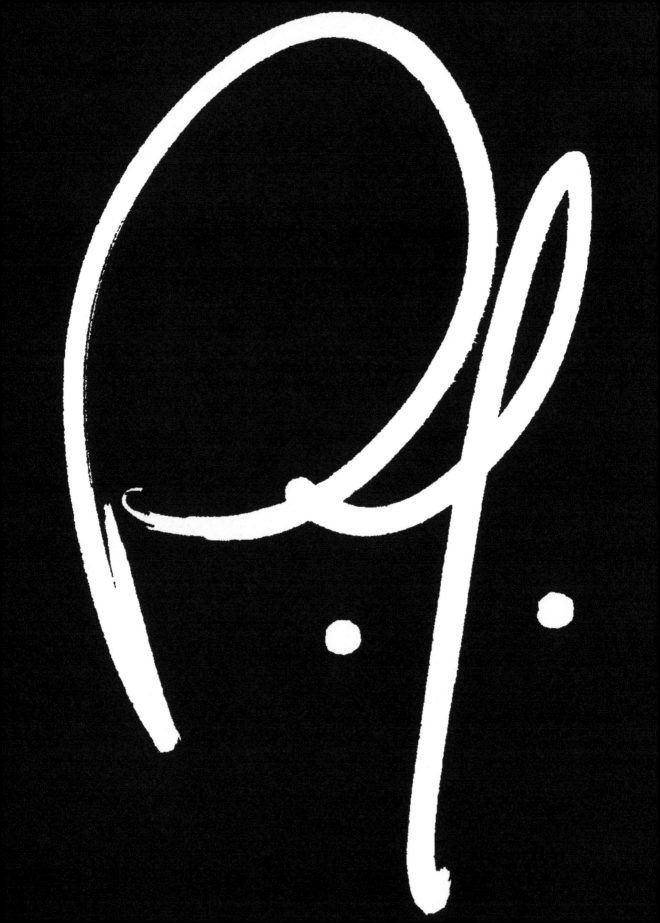

MUSIC
BIOGRAPHY

MUSIC BIOGRAPHY

Paul Anthony Young was born January 17th 1956. He was the middle child of three, has an elder brother Mark and a younger sister Joanne. His interest in music dates back to when he was very young, when he learnt to play the piano and then the guitar. On leaving school he worked with his father for Vauxhall Motors and played in various bands at night. He played bass guitar in his first band but eventually lack of demand for bass players led him back to his first passion, singing. These were lean times musically because his preferred style of music; Soul, was not particularly popular. However he managed to sing in various bands such as Kat Kool & The Kool Kats and later in the better known Street band.

In December of '79 the Street band broke up and Paul went on to form the Q-Tips. During the next two years Paul introduced himself to more and more of the British public through the Q-Tips extensive touring playing 700 shows all over the UK. This period of intense activity gave Paul the chance to develop his unique voice and stage persona. The Q-Tips went their separate ways at the end of 82' and Paul signed as a solo artist with CBS/SONY Records.

Paul really came into his own with a formidably accomplished solo debut album, "NO PARLEZ" released in 83' and including the number one single "Wherever I Lay My Hat" which maintained the number 1 spot for most of that summer followed by "Come Back And Stay" which maintained Paul's presence at the top of the charts.

With the release of his second album "The Secret Of Association" and the success of "Every Time You Go Away" his status as a world star was confirmed.

In 1987 Paul recorded his third album "Between Two Fires" in Milan where he met the Italian singer Zucchero. They became good friends and were later to collaborate very successfully.

MUSIC BIOGRAPHY

One of the highlights of the 1989 'Nelson Mandela Tribute Concert" was Paul's performance of the Crowded House song "Don't Dream It's All Over" which he later recorded for his best of album.

There followed a period of time out to be with his growing family followed by time spent in America where he was to record in Los Angeles and New York the material for his fourth album "Other Voices".

In 1991 Paul recorded a duet with his friend Zucchero on the soon to be worldwide popular "Sensa Una Donna" which along with the aforementioned "Don't Dream It's All Over" were featured on his best of album "From Time To Time".

1992 was spent touring the world, which culminated in Paul's wonderful appearance at the Freddie Mercury Tribute Concert singing "Radio Gaga" and the release of what turned out to be his final album for Sony "The Crossing". Working with the producer Don Was on the material for "The Crossing", Paul was exploring new styles of music, the gulf between the musical past and future had begun to seem impossible to bridge. The single "Otis Blue" from this album would be the last hit single with Sony. Once freed from his contract Paul took time out to take a breath and to reflect, "Every artist wants to change, every record company wants them to stay the same".

Too in love with performing to simply sit around and wait until he had new material to perform. Paul responded to the hiatus in his career by calling up friends and suggesting they get together in an informal group, simply for fun. The result has been Los Pacaminos, surely one of the most accomplished bar bands the London area has ever seen. For the past six years, the seven-strong line-up has been playing publicly two or three times a month, transforming favoured pubs into Tex-Mex haunts for the night purely by their musical presence. "It's total escapism", says Paul. We feature an accordion player, pedal steel, lots of harmonies - which I get to join in on, 'cos I'm just one of five other guys that can all sing lead. It's drinking music really, which suits me fine".

MUSIC BIOGRAPHY

During 1996 Paul prepared new material with long time collaborator, singer songwriter Drew Barfield, he set about assembling a collection of songs which became the self-titled album "Paul Young". This was full of introspective, storyline songs inspired by Paul's trips to the SouthWest of America.

The "Paul Young" album was released on the East-West label in May of '97. Although the single "I Wish You Love" received tremendous support from radio Paul was unhappy with the overall promotion of the album. "I'm older, I'm less inclined to compromise and I have been determined to evolve as an artist", he says. "Now, I'm no longer content to be just the singer. I need to be in control of the whole package".

To further this aim and to develop his songwriting Paul has been working with various songwriters in Nashville, this along with his continuing working relationship with Drew Barfield have produced various cover versions of their songs among them being "Then There's You" by The Wilkinsons and "Tularosa" by Ray Vega.

Early in 1999 saw Paul getting together again with his friends in "Los Pacaminos". They recorded a four track CD-ep that found it's way into London's only Country music station and their self-penned song "Shadows On The Rise" was played on heavy rotation for three months. Paul, "Obviously, we're now planning an album!"

During the summer of '99, Paul undertook a tour of smaller intimate venues across the UK. Performing new and old material with stripped down arrangements built around his voice and acoustic guitar with piano, accordion and backing vocals provided by long time musical collaborator Matt Irving.

"Los Pacaminos" album entitled "In All Their Glory" was released April 2002.

MUSIC BIOGRAPHY

In 2006, with the help of producer Dieter Falk and uber-arrangers Steve Sidwell and Simon Clark, Paul released a Swing Album for the German, Austrian and Swiss markets entitled "Rock Swings – On the Wild Side of Swing" This was released in the USA in early 2010.

Paul continues to write, record and play live. He is breaking new ground each year. In 2009 he toured Israel, New Zealand and Croatia for the first time, amongst the many other countries he regularly visits. These dates were in support of the "No Parlez 25th Anniversary Edition" re-release of his first Solo Album….

During the last couple of years also saw Paul enter another field of endeavour, the world of cooking. The opportunity to appear with his friend Marco Pierre White on his television show "Hell's Kitchen" could not be turned down!

This led to Paul appearing on various TV Cook Shows such as "Saturday Kitchen" hosted by James Martin who accompanied Paul along with "The Hairy Bikers" on a Charity Fun Ride on their respective assortment of motorcycles.

Paul has also appeared at several food trade shows, hosted & cooked for 80 people for a pre show dinner at the O2 Arena prior to a Rod Stewart show.

Paul continues to perform with various friends & configurations of musicians. During 2011 Paul was invited to participate in a series of shows in Denmark organized by Jesper Mortensen (drummer extraordinaire) which went very well & Paul has continued to work with Jesper & his group of musicians on various dates throughout Europe.

2012 is shaping up to be a busy year for Paul with various shows throughout the year with visits to Russia, Italy, Israel and Germany on the schedule. Paul will also be in the studio working with Producer Arthur Baker on an album of songs.

ALBUMS

No Parlez (1983)

The Secret of Association (1985)

Between Two Fires (1986)

Other Voices (1990)

From Time to Time - The Singles Collection (1991)

The Crossing (1993)

Reflections (1994)

Paul Young (1997)

The Essential Paul Young (2003)

No Parlez 25th. Anniversary Edition (2005)

Rock Swings (2006)

SINGLES

Iron Out The Rough Spots (1982)

Love Of The Common People (1982)

Wherever I Lay My Hat (That's My Home) (1983)

Come Back And Stay (1983)

Love Of The Common People (1983)

I'm Gonna Tear Your Playhouse Down (1984)

Everything Must Change (1984)

Every Time You Go Away (1985)

Tomb Of Memories (1985)

Wonderland (1986)

Some People (1986)

Why Does A Man Have To Be Strong? (1987)

Softly Whispering I Love You (1990)

Oh Girl (1990)

Heaven Can Wait (1990)

Calling You (1991)

Senza una donna (Without a Woman) (1991)

Both Sides Now (1991)

Don't Dream It's Over (1991)

What Becomes of the Brokenhearted (1991)

Now I Know What Made Otis Blue (1993)

Hope In A Hopeless World (1993)

It Will Be You (1994)

That's How Heartaches Are Made (1994)

Grazing in the grass (1995)

I Wish You Love (1997)

Ball and Chain (1997)

Make Someone Happy (1997)

food index

Take control

Sort out your finances effortlessly, with our face-to-face advice.

✳ Mortgages

✳ Life insurance

✳ Will Writing

✳ Inheritance Tax Planning

✳ Investments

✳ Pensions

01637 853153

www.karrekfinancial.com

karrek
FINANCIAL

9 Hilgrove Road, Newquay, Cornwall, TR7 2QY

Proud Supporters of 'Recipes Found On My Travels'

ISLAND
ISLAND
ILPS 9188
FREE
SLD3
CHR 1383
CHR 1417 FUN BOY THREE WAITING
THE FUN BOY THREE
ISLD 4
TAMLA MOTOWN
TAMLA MOTOWN
TAMLA MOTOWN
PRO #6
TAMLA
TAMLA
5295 ML2
CBS
MOTOWN
CBS 26783
CBS 26239
Gerry Goffin and Carole King
CONNOISSEUR COLLECTION
CBS
CBS 32726
CHR 1193
UAS 30101
GAP BAND III
I'M STILL IN LOVE WITH YOU
DONNY HATHAWAY LIVE
CBS
TRIP PL871196
WYNONIE HARRIS
DARYL HALL - THREE HEARTS IN THE HAPPY ENDING MACHINE
ROCK-MR BLUES

KOSSOFF KIRKE TETSU RABBIT
FREE
ELLA FITZGERALD/DREAM DANCING
SLIM GAILLARD
HOW SWEET IT IS TO BE LOVED BY YOU — MARVIN GAYE
MARVIN GAYE
THE SONGS OF MARVIN GAYE
What's Going On Marvin Gaye
FREE MY DEAR
MARVIN GAYE ANTHOLOGY
MARVIN GAYE
MARVIN GAYE
MARVIN GAYE
MARVIN GAYE — DREAM OF A LIFETIME
MARVIN GAYE · MIDNIGHT LOVE
MARVIN GAYE
ROMANTICALLY YOURS
GOFFIN AND KING SONGBOOK
OTHER VOICES
GENERATION X - VALLEY OF THE DOLLS
ERROLL GARNER
IMPERIAL ROCKABILLIES
SPOTLIGHT ON AL GREEN SPOT 1016
GWEN GUTHRIE · GOOD TO GO LOVER
AL GREEN
HAIRCUT 100 · PELICAN WEST

FREE / FIRE AND WATER
HEARTBREAKER
FREE AT LAST
THE FREE STORY
THE FREE STORY / Limited Canadian Edition.
PABLO RECORDS 2310 814
"DIANA & MARVIN"
DIANA ROSS & MARVIN GAYE
MARVIN GAYE & TAMMI TERRELL GREATEST HITS
MARVIN GAYE & HIS GIRLS
MARVIN GAYE * M·P·G·

ILPS 9120
ILPS 9217
ILPS 9192
ISLAND RECORDS LTD 1973
ISLAND RECORDS LTD 1973
PRINTED IN UK
HEP 28 Mono
STML 11
STML 11171
STMS 5033
CBS
CBS
CBS-5017
STEREO
STEREO
VSOP LP 34
AL GREEN
© 1972 CHRYSALIS RECORDS LIMITED. PRINTED IN UK
ATCO SD 33-386
RLC 103

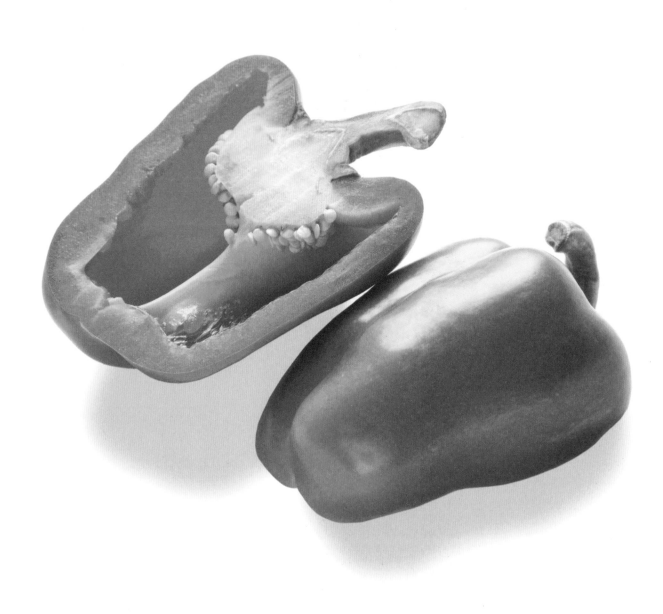